BEAUTY and the BEST

Beneth Peters Jones

BOB JONES UNIVERSITY PRESS

GREENVILLE, SOUTH CAROLINA 29614

Beauty and the Best
by Beneth Peters Jones
© 1980, 1983 Bob Jones University Press
Greenville, South Carolina 29614

Printed in the United States of America
94   93   92   91   90   89   88   87   86   6   5   4

ISBN 0-89084-123-3

Library of Congress Cataloging-in-Publication Data

Jones, Beneth Peters, 1937-
    Beauty and the best.

    1. Women—Religious life. 2. Beauty, Personal.
3. Etiquette for women. I. Title.
BV4527.J66   1986   646.7'04   86-21008
ISBN 0-89084-123-3

For our daughter,
Roxane

Table of Contents

1. The Finest Femininity   *1*
2. Basics for Beauty   *9*
3. Oh—That Oval!   *29*
4. Grace: -Ful or -Less   *53*
5. The Significant Silhouette   *69*
6. Closet Clues   *81*
7. That Awesome Audio   *105*
8. The Manners Message   *123*
9. To Close and Clinch   *149*

Acknowledgments

From its prompting by Christian women across the country who said, "There ought to be a book . . ." to its completion, *Beauty and the Best* has become a reality only through the efforts of many people. I am sincerely and lastingly grateful for their vital contributions. Julia Hansen, Guye Johnson, and Sandy Summers painstakingly read and critiqued the first manuscript. Jim Brooks, Julia Hansen, and Lou Ann Keiser designed the layout. Special thanks is due Julia Hansen, my editor, for her knowledgeable and patient tutoring in the realities of publication processes, and to Jim Brooks for the art work with which he so beautifully translates concepts into visuals. It would likewise be sheer ingratitude to overlook the patience of my husband and children as they endured three years of pencil-chewing and typewriter-banging. And, finally, a loving thank-you to my father-in-law, Dr. Bob Jones, who suggested the title.

BEAUTY and the BEST

The Finest Femininity

The twentieth century Christian girl or woman exists in a spiritually-foreign environment: a world shadowed by sin's darkness; a world where the bizarre is applauded and the beautiful is ridiculed; where earth's inhabitants bear out God's prophetic description:

> For men shall be lovers of their own selves, covetous, boasters, proud, blasphemers, disobedient to parents, unthankful, unholy, Without natural affection, truce-breakers, false accusers, incontinent, fierce, despisers of those that are good, Traitors, heady, high-minded, lovers of pleasures more than lovers of God.   (II Timothy 3:2-4)

One of the most distressing characteristics of our age is the rapid demise of femininity.

Ungodly females have so shouted, belittled, and militated against woman's "slavish" lot that many throughout the land—including Christian women—are asking themselves if femininity—and its enjoyment—really is passe'.

The vital fact to remember in the midst of all the claims, catcalls, and confusion is that *God has not changed His mind*. As He designed femininity, so He desires femininity. Have you noticed that the concept which brings on the worst fits of fury in women's libbers is that woman's role is God-ordained? It is, therefore, *against God Himself* that the "women's liberation" tirade is ultimately aimed. That fact identifies the "women's lib" movement and its philosophies as something to be rejected by those who know and love God through His Son Jesus Christ.

Amid destructive, disheartening surroundings, where can a Christian woman or girl look for a valid standard of feminine identity? To the same place the libbers look in hatred: to God Himself. He who made us also motivates us toward the ideal womanhood seen in precept and example throughout His Word.

But can we be *happy* in the "confines" of femininity, you ask? Supremely so! For there and *only* there can we find the genuine freedom to be and to do all that the Lord intended for women. This truth is written unmistakably upon the faces of the very women who deny it most vehemently: disillusionment and bitterness result from disregarding the Almighty's verities.

The highest level of ladylike sensitivity, appearance, and conduct: that should be the goal of every Christian woman. How dare we do less for our Creator, Redeemer, and King? To settle for less than the finest femininity is to be a thief several times over:

—We rob God of the fulfillment of His perfect plan.

—We rob other women of an inspirational, gracious touch and example.

—We rob the men around us of the opportunity to exercise the protective, gentlemanly considerations native to their masculinity.

—We rob ourselves of the beauty possible only in conformity to divine will.

Before progressing further, let me clearly identify my intended audience. It consists, quite simply, of women everywhere who possess *genuine* internal beauty. That beauty is possible only through sin's cleansing by the shed blood of Jesus Christ and the continuing "housework" of the indwelling Holy Spirit.

Opinions and creeds, labels and deeds don't count for a thing. God's Holy Word, the Bible, makes clear that human beings are helpless to cleanse their own hearts, to purify their own lives; any such futile efforts are, in the sight of an eternal, holy God, a pitiful wrapping in unutterably filthy rags:

> But we are all as an unclean thing, and all our righteousnesses are as filthy rags; and we all do fade as a leaf; and our

iniquities, like the wind, have taken us
away.   (Isaiah 64:6)

Wash you, make you clean; put away the
evil of your doings from before mine
eyes; cease to do evil.   (Isaiah 1:16)

Come now, and let us reason together,
saith the Lord: though your sins be as
scarlet, they shall be as white as snow;
though they be red like crimson, they
shall be as wool.   (Isaiah 1:18)

Perhaps you don't like to acknowledge your
sinfulness; the Bible silences any objections by
saying,

For all have sinned, and come short of the
glory of God.   (Romans 3:23)

Rather than deny them, God calls upon
us to *acknowledge* the filth of our sins and to bring
them to Him for cleansing:

If we confess our sins, he is faithful and
just to forgive us our sins, and to cleanse
us from all unrighteousness.

(I John 1:9)

Why ask God to remove our sins? Because
otherwise a totally righteous, holy, and just
God must condemn our sin and punish it:

For the wages of sin is death; but the gift
of God is eternal life through Jesus
Christ our Lord.   (Romans 6:23)

When we acknowledge and confess our sins, God cancels our punishment because Jesus Christ took our sinfulness upon Himself and died in our behalf on the cross of Calvary. As He cancels our sin debt, He simultaneously extends an eternal gift:

> For by grace are ye saved through faith; and that not of yourselves: it is the gift of God: Not of works, lest any man should boast. (Ephesians 2:8,9)
>
> He that believeth on the Son of God hath the witness in himself: he that believeth not God hath made him a liar; because he believeth not the record that God gave of his Son. And this is the record, that God hath given us eternal life, and this life is in his Son. He that hath the Son hath life; and he that hath not the Son of God hath not life. (I John 5:10-12)
>
> That if thou shalt confess with thy mouth the Lord Jesus, and shalt believe in thine heart that God hath raised him from the dead, thou shalt be saved. For with the heart man believeth unto righteousness; and with the mouth confession is made unto salvation. For whosoever shall call upon the name of the Lord shall be saved. (Romans 10:9, 10, 13)

Saved! Cleansed! Made new by the power of God through the precious blood of His only begotten Son, the sinless Lord Jesus Christ! Sin's stain washed out of the repentant heart, and the

golden tide of God's unspeakable peace sweep-
ing into that heart!

> Therefore being justified by faith, we
> have peace with God through our Lord
> Jesus Christ.   (Romans 5:1)

Only with a heart made clean and lovely by
salvation can a woman move toward genuine
beauty of self and life.

So. Beauty: what is it? Is it the same as *pretti-
ness*? No. The first definition given by Webster is,
"the quality attributed to whatever pleases or
satisfies the senses or mind, as by line, color,
form, texture, proportion, rhythmic motion,
tone, etc., or by behavior, attitude, etc." That's a
much broader definition than we ordinarily hold
in our feminine minds, isn't it? What a tremendous encouragement to every one of us.
Proverbs 31 reminds us that beauty in and of
itself is "vain" (empty and meaningless). But so is
virtually *every* attribute and accomplishment of
human beings, the writer of Ecclesiastes
reminds us, if it is pursued for its own sake. On
the other hand, beauty is a worthy goal for every
Christian woman if we (a) recognize that our
soul has been made beautiful by our altogether
lovely Lord, (b) desire discernible beauty as
demonstrative of His original design in creating
femininity, and (c) seek to be reflectors of His
beautiful holiness.

Having thus defined my intended audience
and established a scripturally-acceptable ratio-

nale, let me state my intended purpose in writing this book:

To encourage and assist born-again Christian women of any age toward the cultivation of feminine loveliness in every outward aspect of self and life, in order to reflect the beauty Jesus Christ has given to soul and heart.

In order to offer practical application and assistance, Chapters Two through Eight are followed by "Personal Pinpointing" sheets. These are designed to help you recognize and analyze where you are and what you need with regard to the various subjects discussed. These can be handled in a private, class, or friend-shared fashion.

Lest at any point we should lose sight of the book's purpose, the following chapters will also end with what I've chosen to call a "Spiritual Balance." This is a scripturally-based reminder of those spiritual considerations which must underlie the physical, material, and behavioral principles being dealt with by that particular chapter. These are matters which the unsaved world would never consider—but which the saved woman or girl must never forget!

2

Basics for Beauty

Meticulous grooming, knowledgeable use of cosmetics and clothing, graceful carriage, impeccable manners and pleasing speech—all are wasted motion if we overlook nutrition and good health. Therefore, before dealing with the principles of good grooming, it's fitting to mention a few principles of good health.

It is impossible to look good if you don't feel well. No matter how busy and demanding your life, Christian woman, your good health should be foundational in your self (and family!) care.

What a marvelous creation the human body is—yet how careless we are in tending it. Those of us who know the God Who created our bodies should be attentive to the care of those bodies.

Volumes have been written on the subject of nutrition—and I would urge you to check a couple of them out of your local library and brush up on the subject. A balanced diet is essential both to your pleasing appearance and to your positive energy quotient.

Briefly, let me remind you of the main food groups:

Milk and milk products—Utilized for building/maintaining teeth and bones. High, however, in animal fats.

Meat, fish, and eggs—sources of protein; beef and pork products highest in fats; fowl and fish lowest.

Fruits and vegetables—high in vitamin and mineral content; helpful in providing roughage.

Grains and cereals—wide-ranging in types, texture, and taste; especially important in providing fiber content.

Rather than recommending any particular approach to nutrition, I would instead urge a general, common-sense approach including the following suggestions:

Have a complete physical examination by your doctor, and solicit his advice about certain foods for your individual needs.

Avoid dietary extremes. Don't let yourself become a "food nut" in any sense of the word. Most of us have had the unpleasant experience of being accosted by "nutrition evangelists." Overemphasis in the matter of foods is a favorite trick of the devil to sidetrack believers from proper *spiritual* fervor. The Bible specifically warns against those who recommend dietary extremes!

Be faithful in visiting your physician and

dentist as often as they recommend: preventive measures are wiser and more pleasant than curative ones.

Get plenty of rest. God has so constructed our bodies that we have definite sleep requirements. These vary from person to person, but the average amount of sleep needed in a 24-hour period is six to eight hours. Whatever the amount best for *your* peak functioning, be sure that you generally get it. Consistently driving yourself on less rest than you need is courting physical, emotional, and even spiritual disaster. The components of our beings are closely intertwined: neglect or abuse in one area damages the others as well.

Besides the sleep you get at night, learn the value of a daytime nap. You can train yourself to fall asleep very quickly—and a ten- to thirty-minute nap can do wonders for your emotional and physical stamina! Skimping on sleep not only shows up today in dark-circled eyes and dragging steps, it also makes a daily deposit in the bank of premature aging.

Recognize exercise as an important contributor to good health. It not only aids in maintaining good muscle tone, but also encourages the efficient functioning of our internal systems.

Drink plenty of water. Six to eight glasses of liquid daily is a good goal. Unglamorous though it may be, water is *the* most important intake-item for maintaining the intricate cleansing system the Lord has built into our bodies.

Having touched upon those few basic considerations having to do with your good health, let's go on now to discuss good grooming.

Just as reputable merchants make sure that the windows in which they display their goods are well-washed, so we who seek to direct attention to our lovely Lord must be consistently careful about cleanliness, because *the Christian woman should be an attractive show-window for her Saviour and Lord*. Therefore, there is absolutely no excuse for a dirty Christian! Isaiah reminds us:

> Be ye clean, that bear the vessels of the Lord.   (Isaiah 52:11)

Cleanliness is foundational to any discussion of personal appearance. If you are not scrupulously *clean* about your person and clothing, any interest in, effort toward, or program for self-improvement will be doomed to failure.

Specifically, scour-and-polish efforts need to be exerted upon all the "surfaces"—skin, hair, nails, teeth, and clothing.

SKIN

Sometimes we think of ourselves as having skin only on our faces; but of course it covers our entire earthly tabernacle, and we must give it the best of care—beginning with thorough cleansing.

If you tend to shrug your shoulders about your skin, take a few moments to read about the wonders of human skin in a good encyclopedia. You may be greatly surprised: that much-abused, taken-for-granted "hide" you carry around is actually a marvelous, intricate part of God's human creation. If His concern in creating us was so detailed, shouldn't our stewardship be similarly painstaking?

Keep your skin—all of it—*clean*. That means daily-or-oftener scrubbing. Skin is a living organism, a working part of the body. As it labors to maintain body temperature and to protect the delicate internal mechanism, it exudes moisture. That moisture, combined with any body dirt or soiled clothing, and warmed by the skin itself, produces a distinctive, unpleasant aroma: the well-advertised "B.O."—body odor.

Remember that *all* of your skin is working and leaving odor-producing deposits. So a dab of deodorant here, a splash of cologne there, will *not* result in aromatic sweetening! The only way to eliminate odor is to eliminate its cause: in other words, wash off the skin's secretions. Daily cleansing with soap and water is available to, inexpensive for, and *demanded of* any woman who desires to be a spiritual magnet.

Briefly imagine yourself an unsaved person. Would you be attracted to the religion of someone exuding body odor?

Another reason for bathing daily is to remove the sloughed-off cells your skin discards as it consistently renews itself.

There are some places on the body that demand special cleaning attention—areas where structure and/or enclosure contribute to the creation and containment of odor:

Feet Underarms Genital area	These must be scrupulously scrubbed at least once daily, *and* deodorized as needed. It's not a matter of "either-or"—modern anti-perspirants and deodorants are a boon to all who desire to be well-groomed.

Also, some areas of the body need special attention because of their exposure to pressure, surfaces, and elements:

Hands Elbows Knees Heels	The rougher, tougher skin in these areas demands more than a once-over-lightly to insure the removal of staining, clinging dirt.

Since these are areas that also tend toward roughness, by all means be liberal in softening efforts such as soaking and creaming.

Now we come to that particular skin-covered patch we're all so familiar with—the face. And as with the rest of the body, here too the basic principle to be observed is *cleanliness*. No matter how you may back-pedal or bluster, *blackheads are not beautymarks!*

Generally speaking, women in their thirties, forties, and on up recognize the importance of good skin care. The sad fact is, though, in many cases they've been slow to come to that recognition: the carelessness of youth is paid for in maturity. Ideally, a girl should learn good skin-cleansing habits as soon as she's old enough to hold a washcloth.

In cleansing the face, we must first of all consider the *type skin* which covers its planes and hollows. There are three basic facial skin types: dry, normal, and oily. There are also combinations of types on one face. That is, your skin may be basically normal but have oily areas on forehead, nose, and chin. If you have facial skin that's all one type, use the cleansing method best suited to it. If your facial skin combines two or even all three of the types, resign yourself to a varied cleansing routine. Whatever the method, the important thing is to keep your skin clean—*clean*—CLEAN!

The methods of cleansing best suited to the different skin types are as follows:

Normal	Soap and water, twice daily
Dry	Cleansing cream and/or special soaps, post-scrub creaming; twice daily
Oily	Soap and water (perhaps with specially-formulated soap), use of a face brush or sponge; astringent; twice or more daily

Whenever soap and water is applied to the face, be sure *all* soap is completely rinsed away. Soap residues clog pores and attract dirt.

Drying your face should always be done by patting rather than by rubbing.

Never fall into the trap of thinking "another coat of makeup will fix it." Start fresh! You'll not only look better, but you'll also feel better after cleansing your face.

A final consideration in skin hygiene is the regular removal of hair from underarms, face, and legs. Hairiness is unsightly and unacceptable for a lady. Hair can be removed from legs and underarms by razor or depilatory. Facial hair should *never* be shaved, but may be removed either by depilatory preparations created specifically for facial use or by electrolysis.

HAIR

All the styling in the world can't beautify hair that isn't clean. As in the case of skin, hair comes in three basic types: dry, normal, and oily. There are shampoos made for each one of the types; you would be wise to buy with that fact in mind. It's easy to be a bit dazzled by the wide array of shampoo choices lining the shelves of a drugstore. But don't be bamboozled by either advertising or price tags. You're looking for a shampoo "built" for your kind of hair. Catchy advertising jingles aren't going to help your hair at all; neither is a hefty price tag or high-fallutin' manufacturers' names on the label. Simply buy the shampoo that will do the most for your hair for the least expense. After a bit of experimenting, stick with the one you find.

Once you've decided on the best shampoo for your needs, then decide what frequency is best for keeping your hair at its peak in appearance. Oily hair may need to be washed every day, whereas dry hair may need only a weekly shampoo. Whatever the ideal cleanliness-care schedule for your hair, make that schedule a habit and hold to it. Don't yield to the temptation to get by just one extra day before shampooing. You're not the only one who'll know! That extra day of dirt-gathering will be evident to those around you.

I've always found it interesting that men and women think differently about hair beauty. To a woman, beautiful hair is primarily a matter of style and color; to a man, however, hair is beautiful when it's *shiningly clean*. Herein we women need to acknowledge the greater wisdom of our men! Too often we concentrate on the "metallics" of our crowning glory rather than on its *material*. The ideal, of course, is to maintain hair that is both squeaky-clean and flatteringly styled.

The most important step of the actual shampoo is the rinse. If you want shining hair, be sure to do a thorough rinse job every time. Any residual shampoo dulls the shine and attracts dirt like a magnet. If you have difficulty removing shampoo from your hair, try "cutting" the suds with a lemon juice-and-water mixture (for blonds) or a vinegar-and-water solution (for brunettes). After several water-only rinsings, pour the mixture through your hair, then rinse again with clean water. *Shine* will result!

NAILS

Nails are a distinctive type of surface God made for our bodies. These hard protectors at the ends of fingers and toes are much more functional than we ordinarily realize. If a nail is ripped back deeply into the quick, or torn off completely, we are instantly convinced that toenails and fingernails are important! Our omniscient Heavenly Father installed them as protection and strength for ever-active hands and feet.

Besides being utilitarian, nails are also ornamental. They give a finished, definitive appearance to fingers and toes.

The cleanliness and grooming of nails are important to both their practical and ornamental functions. Hands with dirty fingernails moving to and into the mouth are sure to transport germs. And clean, well-cared-for nails enhance attractiveness—not of hands alone, but also of the entire woman.

Years ago I read of a woman whose face missed beauty by a considerable degree; nevertheless she was considered a beauty—because her hands were flawlessly beautiful in appearance and movement. This woman recognized her hands as her major asset, and she capitalized upon them by giving them meticulous care and by always wearing dresses whose long sleeves and wrist trims called attention to her exquisite hands. Conversely, I can think of women who, despite attractive faces, do not leave the impression of beauty *because of poorly-kept hands.*

Cleanliness, gloss, and shape are the characteristics of well-groomed nails.

Cleanliness is aided by use of a nail brush in handwashing. Also, dirt should be removed from under nails between washings by careful use of a fingernail file.

Gloss is a natural characteristic of healthy nails. It can also be enhanced by oiling and buffing the nails or with clear or natural fingernail polish.

If you use colored nail polish, remember that a Christian woman is wise to avoid garish, super-dark or ultra-bright colors. The "in" look doesn't really matter; our guidelines should be, only and always, the "within" look—within the bounds of subtlety and restraint. It's also "handy" to remember that colored nail polish calls attention to your hands: people will thereby be attracted to notice the size, shape, movements, etc., more than they ordinarily would. And a final word about polish—*never* wear it chipped: chipped fingernail color screams sloppiness!

Shape of nails is attractively maintained by keeping the cuticles pushed back from the inner ends and keeping the outer ends smooth and gently rounded.

There are two unlovely extremes to avoid in the length of fingernails: blunt and misshappen "stubs" from biting/tearing, or over-long "claws." (Nail-biting is an unladylike habit which can—and should—be broken.)

Who among us has the leisurely, unpressurized life to sit around and concentrate on growing perfect fingernails? Nobody! Our hands are constantly busy—and many of our chores make existence difficult for fingernails. But there are some counter-measures we can all manage. If your nails are unsightly because they split and break, two practical aids are wearing rubber gloves for household chores and consuming a packet of unflavored gelatine dissolved in fruit juice once daily.

A daily vitamin supplement can offset any dietary vitamin deficiency which might affect nail growth. There are also some nail strengthening solutions available; they work by absorption into the nail after being brushed on.

Toenails deserve better care than most of us give them. They, too, should be cleaned, shaped, and buffed or polished regularly. Their best length is just to the end of the toe, and relatively straight-cut ends will help avoid the painful problems of ingrown toenails.

TEETH

Considering the millions of dollars spent annually on advertising by the manufacturers of toothpaste and mouthwash, it's a nine-day wonder that *anyone* has to be told of the necessity for good oral hygiene. But sad to say, a hefty number of Christian women apparently think of their mouths solely as food-intake slots. Naturally, such mouths become halitosis-output slots! Bad breath and unbrushed teeth are a surefire method of repulsing people. It is inconceivable that a Christian woman would presume to speak words of testimony from an odorous, food-stained mouth!

Make frequent tooth brushing and mouth washing habitual. For the time spans between, do *not* resort to chewing gum to sweeten your breath! Your motives may be good—but your appearance will instantly drop 75 notches! Not long ago I was freshly impressed by the unlovely effects of gum chewing. My husband and I were sitting in the lobby of a hotel near Chicago waiting to be picked up for an evening church service. Also in the lobby were two young women waiting for a bus. They appeared to be in their 20s, and both of them were beautifully dressed in clothes which were carefully and expensively tailored. But the entire effect of a well-groomed appearance was destroyed— because they were chewing gum ninety-to-nothing!

I challenge you to spend a week watching female gum-chewers. If you're honest, you will admit before the week is ended that the jaw-jiggling habit plunges a woman's appearance into the minus bracket.

So you're worried lest you offend with bad breath? That's a valid concern—but gum is not the solution. There is no shortage of breath-sweeteners on the market—mouthwashes, sprays, drops, mints, etc.—any one of which eliminates any "need" for chewing gum. And if you don't care for any of those, here's a personal tip (remembered from my grandmother): keep a whole clove in your mouth. It will last for hours, and an occasional gentle squeeze with your teeth will release a fresh spicy essence.

CLOTHING

As with the body, so too with clothing: *cleanliness* should be the Christian woman's primary consideration. Most of us who are rich in eternal holdings lack in earthly wealth; a thin purse, however, is no excuse for skimping on neatness. Some of the best-dressed Christian women I've known through the years have *not* been those with plenty of money and closets full of clothes. But without exception they've been women who practiced scrupulous sartorial neatness. One freshly-washed, perfectly-pressed dress is better than ten with stains, odor, and wrinkles! Clothes collect soil very quickly when they're worn—not only from contact with externals, but also from contact with the body. You simply can't be too careful, therefore, in insuring that your clothing is clean.

Washable garments should be laundered according to attached fabric instructions *after every wearing*. That includes panties, bras, and other out-of-sight wear. For outer wear, be leery of accepting "permanent press" labels at face value. More often than not, to make such clothing really look its best you must press with a steam iron after the piece comes from the dryer. Almost-smooth should not be considered good enough—after all, it's not the *size* of the wrinkles that count, but their *presence*.

Woolen clothing presents a different cleaning problem. Because of the high cost of dry cleaning, it's usually impractical to clean after every wearing. Therefore, your special care of wools during and after wear is critically important.

The wisest protection you can provide for any wool outfit is to wear underarm shields. You can't count on 100% effectiveness from *any* deodorant, and even a tiny bit of perspiration on wool is devastating.

Let a wool outfit hang where air can circulate freely through it for an hour or two after each wearing. *Don't* stuff the garment back into your closet immediately. After its airing, be sure to make a thorough, careful inspection: if there is any sign of griminess or odor, send the outfit to the cleaners. Expensive is better than *offensive*!

The neatness of your clothing during wear depends upon your concern for accurate fit. Seams should rest *exactly* in their intended places—not a half inch east, west, north, or south. Waistline and shoulder seams are the greatest offenders in this regard; but vertical seams, too, must receive attention. Whether you purchase or make your clothes, insist on precise fit. A narrow-shouldered woman wearing a dress with shoulder seams hanging halfway to

her elbows can't hope for a neat appearance.
Neither can a long-waisted woman look neat if
the waistline of her dress rides her midriff. Both
these examples are exaggerated to make a point
for the importance of accurate "lay" in seams.
Get an unshakable grip on this guideline for
every piece of clothing you wear: *poor fits are
misfits*!

Bras and slips can destroy a neat appearance
in several sneaky ways:

—A slip hanging longer than the hem of the
outerwear.

—A slip too short for a garment (correct
length: just to the top of the outer clothing's
hem).

—A half-slip "crawling" and lumping under
"static-y" fabrics.

—A slip or bra strap falling off the shoulders.

—A half-slip worn under a transparent or
semi-transparent garment. (ALWAYS wear a
full slip under such clothing. No matter how
lightly the unsaved world treats the display of
undergarments, Christians should not.)

Unless you happen to be the one-in-a-
million woman whose frame fits the mythical
"average," you will rarely find ready-made
clothes that are *really* ready—for you. Most of us
find one or more places in a garment where its
measurements don't fit ours. Whether shopping
or sewing, impatience is bound to whisper in
your ear, "Nearly right is good enough!" But if
you are going to look your best for the Lord, you
must consistently answer that whisper, "I'm not

going to settle for anything less than *just* right!" It all boils down to this: misfits not only detract from your appearance; they also detract from your attitude by making you feel uncomfortable, dowdy, and miserable. Therefore, a few clothes that fit perfectly are worth closets full that fit poorly.

What about the total effect of a garment fit-wise? The guiding principle should be God's demand for *modesty*. The woman who sincerely seeks to glorify the Lord by her appearance should always avoid above-the-knee or deeply slit skirts, low necklines, and peek-a-boo clothing. Remember too, though, that a blouse, skirt or dress that clings to the lines of the body is *not* modest, no matter how long the hemline or how high the neckline.

Before leaving home in any outfit, be sure to check your view in a full-length mirror! What looks right in front can look awful in back—especially when you move. Most of us have problems with ups and downs of weight; but when the "ups" make any garment too tight, we should stop wearing the outfit until we've stopped wearing the weight.

Some of us put our clothing out of kilter by what we do to it after we put it on. Pulling a belt too tight, for instance, can make you look like a sausage tied in the middle. Yanking at a skirt hem when seated makes for a sagging hemline.

Maybe in reading this chapter, you think, "I don't have *time* for all this!" But you do—because scrupulous cleanliness and neatness is a matter of *depth* of attention, not *length* of attention. Simply apply intensified effort in every area of your personal grooming. If, however, you've really skimped in the various aspects discussed in this section, you may indeed have to designate a bit more time for grooming.

Or perhaps you react with *guilt* to the idea of taking time for careful grooming. Many Christian women have picked up the notion that *all* time and effort should be spent on others. But, according to God's Word, that's not true. Even the well-known verse, "Thou shalt love thy neighbor as thyself," implies a concern for self—otherwise, it would read, "Thou shalt love thy neighbor *instead of* thyself." Or consider that marvelous virtuous woman of Proverbs 31. There are roughly 18 verses dealing directly with her various attributes and accomplishments. One of those reveals the obvious care she bestows upon herself (verse 22). If we were to translate those 18 verses into hours (about a normal work day's length for any of us), we could safely say that she spends one hour of her day on herself. Without her self-respecting attention to her own well-being and appearance, she might very easily serve others with a martyr's complex or an embittered spirit—either of which would disqualify her for honor!

In summary, then, the overriding control-phrase for a born-again woman's appearance should be MODESTY, CLEANLINESS, AND NEATNESS—ALWAYS.

Personal Pinpointing

1. My most serious nutritional neglect is in the
_____ food group(s).

2. I generally feel at my best when I have had
_____ hours of sleep at night.

3. My present exercise level would most accurately be classified as:

Superior   Good   Average   Below average

4. I should consume _____ more glasses of liquid daily in order to reach the proper level of intake.

5. My personal concern for bodily cleanliness would probably be classified:

Meticulous   Average   Needs improvement

6. I believe my skin is _____ in type. That means I should be using the _____ cleansing method.

7. Because my hair is the _____ type, I need to wash it _____ times a week. The best scheduling for shampoos is _____ (time of day) on _____ (day(s) of the week).

8. The condition and appearance of my fingernails (enhances/detracts from) a well-groomed look.

9. This chapter has reminded me that I need to begin or stop _____ for the sake of oral hygiene.

10. I should be more careful about _____ in my clothes care and wear routine.

Spiritual Balance

Why is good grooming important to a Christian woman? Because it is an outward reflection of the inner reality of her salvation. There are no smudges, tears, or sagging hems on the beautiful garment of salvation as it comes from the hand of the Lord Jesus Christ. Nor does heaven, the eternal home toward which we journey, contain anything but that which is perfect, clean, and bright. Because an eternal God cared enough about the cleanliness of our soul to pay the unutterable price of His only Son's blood, the housing of our immortal souls should surely be the object of our best, our most careful and consistent grooming efforts.

3

Oh–That Oval!

A face. (Clean, of course!) That fascinating, roughly oval expanse of tissue and tones, bony planes and fleshy hollows by which the Lord has depicted our identity, character, and personality as well as framing our view of the world.

For a woman, added to the need for identity is the built-in desire for comeliness. That desire, when properly channeled and controlled, is legitimate. The yearning for personal beauty was placed within the feminine nature by God Himself: it is only the *abuse* or *misuse* of that yearning that dishonors Him. How can anyone sensibly contend that the Altogether Lovely One is honored by a feminine face deliberately or ignorantly made unlovely?

More important than your artistry with your face is your attitude toward it. Study your countenance in the mirror. Have you *accepted* it—

good points and not-so-good—as being the one
the Lord wanted you to have? If not, you're
sinning against the Lord—for you are dissatis-
fied with the way He made you:

> Woe unto him that striveth with his
> Maker! Let the potsherd strive with the
> potsherds of the earth. Shall the clay say
> to him that fashioneth it, What makest
> thou? or thy work, He hath no hands?
> (Isaiah 45:9)

There is neither accident nor mistake in the way
you were formed, Christian woman. You are a
special, pre-known creation:

> Thine eyes did see my substance, yet
> being unperfect; and in thy book all my
> members were written, which in con-
> tinuance were fashioned, when as yet
> there was none of them. (Psalm 139:16)

Or, conversely, are you sinning against God by
being proud of your face? Pride disfigures the
soul and thereby debases facial beauty. It doesn't
even make sense for you to get puffed-up over
something that came as a gift of the Lord!

> For who maketh thee to differ from
> another? and what hast thou that thou
> didst not receive? now if thou didst
> receive it, why dost thou glory, as if thou
> hadst not received it? (I Corinthians 4:7)

Once you have come to simple acceptance of
your countenance, you can set the goal of doing
the most with what the Lord has given you
facially, via the right kind of attractiveness.

After facial acceptance should come facial analysis. All of us occasionally direct a withering glance at a long nose, a square chin, small eyes, or a large mouth as it is reflected from the mirror. In fact, it's a feminine trait to concentrate on our "bad points" almost to the exclusion of the good ones. Yet everyone *does have* some beauty of feature. The problem is that many women either don't know how or won't take the time to analyze and accentuate their comely facial attributes. Of course, it is upon that word "accentuate" that believers vary so widely in opinion. Let's briefly discuss that divergence: *what about cosmetics?*

Some who staunchly hold the *"No* artifice!" position are actually pretty inconsistent—they condemn a touch of rouge, but gladly adopt false teeth; they decry lip color, but routinely wear shoulder pads or cologne.

Moreover, undue emphasis upon externals is just as wrong on the minus side as it is on the plus side. Of *course* a Christian woman does wrong to paint and posture like a streetwalker. But the proclaimer of "paleness is purity" is likewise off-base. There is no redemptive power in a pale face and knee-length hair! After all, can't you think of individuals, sects and groups whose plain-dress appearance only provides a pathetic camouflage for gross immorality?

In the final analysis, the use or non-use of cosmetics by a Christian woman must be dictated by personal conviction and/or *by your husband's wishes*, married woman.

Personally, I would no more leave my face untended than I'd leave my home unpainted: I feel that either neglect would cause someone to turn away from the Lord with the snorted comment, "Christians certainly are a careless, colorless lot!" You may feel just as strongly that you should not use cosmetics. Fine. But your basic grooming must still demand considerable attention so that your appearance is glowing. *For the believer, cosmetics must be always a subtle enhancer only.*

SKIN

Whereas flawless skin needs no enhancement, even it can well use the protection a good makeup base affords against the elements; and skin that has blemishes of texture or color definitely needs the assistance of base for the sake of appearance. The color of your base should be as near your own skin tone as possible. Apply base *very* lightly and be careful to blend it around the hairline and along the jawbone. There must be no "mask" look due to excessively heavy application or obvious stop/start lines around the edges. A water-soluble base is generally better suited to oily skin, while the oil-base type lends greater assistance to dry skin. To give an extra-natural look to water-soluble base, sponge water onto your entire face after applying base; while skin is damp, gently re-smooth the base, giving special attention to the edges. To eliminate the shiny, waxy look which oil-base foundation can have, blot your entire face with a tissue immediately after applying your foundation.

FACIAL SHAPE

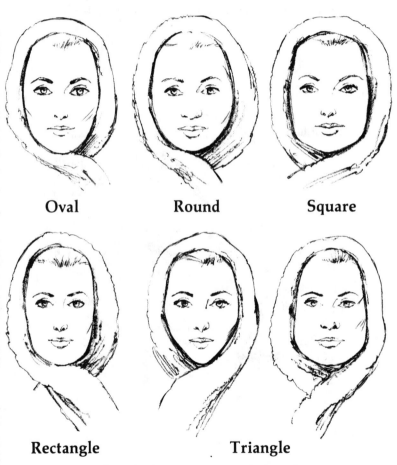

| Oval | Round | Square |

| Rectangle | Triangle |

Your facial shape is one of the above: not *exactly*, of course, but roughly. To determine which one, cover your hair with a towel, thus exposing the true shape of your facial structure. Look squarely into the mirror. If necessary, draw the different facial shapes in soap on your mirror, and move so your face appears inside one

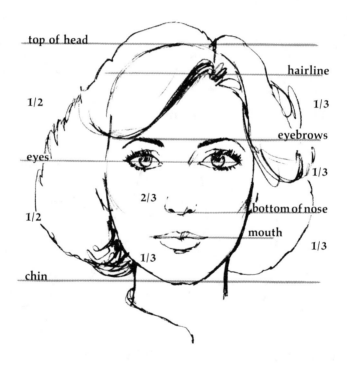

after another of the soap shapes. It may take you several times back and forth before you decide which is most definitely yours. But it's important that you *know* which shape is yours: your goal in both makeup and hair styling will be to *ovalize* your face as much as possible.

PROPORTION

There is also an "ideal" arrangement of facial features. All of us have eyes, nose, and mouth in generally similar locations. But the face that is most pleasing to the eye has its individual features at certain relative distances from each other. It is from this proportional scaling that such terms as "long chin" or "high forehead" arise.

It is with regard to both shape and proportion that the skillful use of cosmetics and hair styling is important. The basic tool for corrective cosmetics is make-up base in three tones: the one best matching your own complexion, a slightly lighter shade, and a slightly darker shade. With these three shades you can "model" the shape of your face.

The basic principle to be applied in correctional modelling is that dark recedes (or minimizes), while light advances (or emphasizes). Therefore, if some area of your face is overly prominent or proportionately unpleasing, you will use the darker tone for correction. Conversely, if there is an area which lacks desirable prominence, length, or width, you will use the lighter.

Following are some examples of corrective base application:

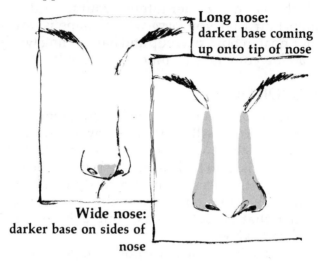

Long nose:
darker base coming up onto tip of nose

Wide nose:
darker base on sides of nose

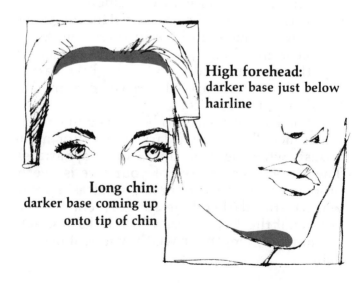

High forehead:
darker base just below hairline

Long chin:
darker base coming up onto tip of chin

A prime requisite of corrective cosmetics is blending. There should never be lines of demarcation where one tone stops and another begins. Blend! Then when you think you've accomplished your goal, check the effect in natural light (daylight, preferably; by all means something *other than* fluorescent), and blend again.

EYES

Eyes are the "windows of the soul"; we who know Christ as Saviour want always to let the spiritual beauty of a blood-cleansed heart shine through those windows. Since eyes are the most direct portals to and indicators of our personality, character, and soul, they should be the focal point of our faces. If you have not been endowed with naturally beautiful eyes and you decide to give them a bit of "help" cosmetically, any such aid should be so delicately applied that it never calls attention to itself, but instead simply and subtly enhances. Remember that our appearance is to reflect the "meek and quiet spirit" Christian women are to have, according to I Peter 3:4. That immediately rules out the brazen, heavy-handed application seen in advertisements!

The characteristics which mark beautiful eyes are size, depth, spacing, and luminosity. In camouflaging less-than-pleasing eye characteristics, carry through with the "lighter for emphasizing, darker for downplaying" principle. Close-set eyes, for example, can be given an appearance "plus" by extending light base onto the sides of the nose between the eyes.

Whatever their natural color, eyebrows should be kept neatly shaped by plucking away stray hairs from underneath. As plucking makes the shape of the brows plainer, it simultaneously makes the eyes appear larger.

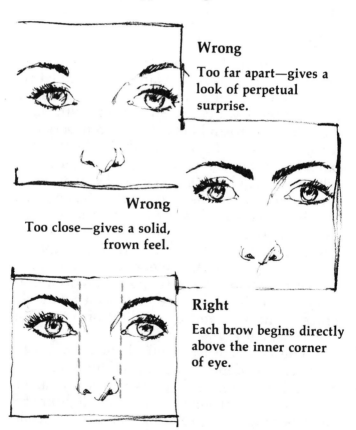

Wrong

Too far apart—gives a look of perpetual surprise.

Wrong

Too close—gives a solid, frown feel.

Right

Each brow begins directly above the inner corner of eye.

Brows differ in natural shape from face to face. In enhancing the appearance of yours, DON'T scrap the original and start all over! Instead, work with the shape and arch natural to your brows. Maybe you're not sure just how much plucking to do, or where. As for "how much," do as little as possible—removing only the "strays" that make the shape indistinct. Perhaps the most important part of the "where" answer has to do with the brows' inner starting point.

Most eyebrows do *not* need to be darkened. Only if yours are pale or scraggly to the point of making your eyes appear brow-less should you use eyebrow pencil. Even then, add to the definition and color of the brows only by very lightly pencilling with lead *closest in color to your natural brow tone.* Use short, light, hair-length strokes of the pencil, with spaces left between strokes. The Lord created eyebrows out of individual hairs; avoid re-making them into one-piece solids via eyebrow pencil.

If your eyelashes do the "hang and hide" routine, curl the upper fringes. Curling not only makes the lashes frame the eye more attractively, but also lends the appearance of enlargement. To obtain a longer-lasting, more natural look than the "curler-bent" one often seen, move the curler two or three times during the curling: that is, tighten it once on the lashes near the roots; loosen, move the curler out toward the lash ends and re-clamp; repeat, even closer to the ends.

Some brunettes have eyelashes which are naturally dark enough to be seen along their entire length. Most of us, though, are not so agreeably endowed. Therefore, to remove lashes from the colorless and nondescript category, you may choose to use mascara. The key word again is *sparingly*. And choose the most subtle color possible for un-obtrusive blending with your natural coloring. If you want to add length to short, stubby lashes, there are good length-building products on the market.

In using *any* mascara, avoid the "glop and top" method of application. Eyelashes were created from delicate individual *hairs* and when they're defined by mascara they should by all means still look like hairs—not like baling wires freshly dipped in creosote!

A parting note on eyelashes: be sure to remove every particle of mascara at the end of a day. Leftover mascara is singularly unlovely, and it has uncanny talent for smudging on cheeks, pillows, and bath linens. Moreover, it serves as an exceedingly poor base for tomorrow morning's fresh application.

EYEGLASSES

Need eyeglasses make your eyes unat-tractive? No! Some of the prettiest eyes I've ever seen have smiled out from behind corrective lenses. Moreover, designers and manufacturers of optical frames are doing great things for making necessities flattering. Wise choice of right design for your face will add an intriguing individuality to your appearance, rather than detract from it. Actually, a woman looks much better in well-chosen glasses than she does in contact lenses if the contacts make her squint, blink, and frown.

CHEEKS

In using rouge, aim for a slight, unobtrusive heightening of cheek pigmentation—*if* you need it. Anything more than a gentle blush on your cheekbones lends hardness to your appearance. Remember, you're a Christian, not a clown! It's also important to blend, blend, *blend* the edges so the blush fades naturally into surrounding skin tone.

LIPS

That lipstick's primary purpose is to intensify color is obvious; however, it can also be used effectively to perfect the shape and proportion of your mouth.

As with all forms of color in cosmetics, stick to *subtlety* of tone in your lipstick choice. Too-darks, too-lights, too-brights, are *too* obvious for a mouth which is to be speaking forth the testimony of the Lord Jesus Christ.

If you use lip color to improve the shape and proportion of your mouth, extend your make-up base onto your lips first. Then proceed, *with the help of a lipstick brush*, to remedy lip imperfections:

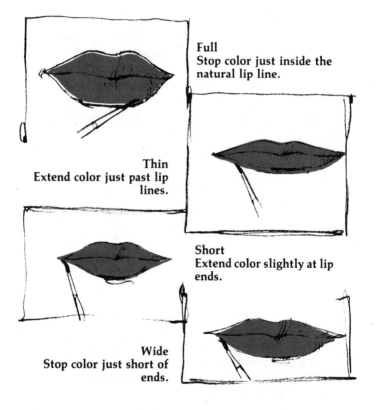

Full
Stop color just inside the natural lip line.

Thin
Extend color just past lip lines.

Short
Extend color slightly at lip ends.

Wide
Stop color just short of ends.

In all shape and size enhancements, be sure that the changes are *very* slight—otherwise they will only call attention to themselves and to the problem you're trying to camouflage.

HAIR

Women are quick to discuss and complain about hair types, characteristics, and styles; most of us, however, don't go very far beyond *just* talking. That's unfortunate, because a woman's hair serves as a frame for her face;

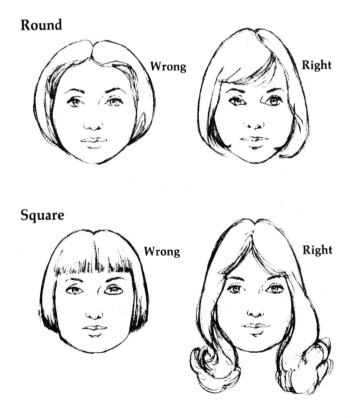

Round

Wrong   Right

Square

Wrong   Right

Long

Wrong   Right

Triangle

Wrong   Right

unwise framing can be one of the stealthiest, most successful thieves of feminine attractiveness.

First of all, consider what type frame your face needs. Correct hair styling can do a great deal to ovalize your face and give the illusion of ideal proportions.

Besides the shape of your face, consider also your height, weight, and body type. Your hairstyle should be in keeping with your overall appearance proportionately:

Tall

Wrong

Right

Athletic

Wrong

Right

Petite

Wrong   **Right**

Whatever style you adopt because of its maximum flattery, *do* start with a good cut. Poorly-cut hair cannot be made to do what you need and want it to do. In looking for a good beautician, it's wiser to ask for one *who handles your type hair well* rather than simply asking for a good stylist. Good hair cutting is not just chopping and lopping; more importantly, it has to do with *shaping*—and different hair textures handle entirely differently under blade or scissors. Before you let the operator touch your hair, tell her exactly what result you want; explain the difficulties you have encountered in styling your hair; get her advice on how to best prepare your hair for styling after its basic cut.

To keep your hair looking its shining, attractive best, be resigned to the fact that you may gradually have to build up quite a shelf-full of hair products, depending on your hair type, such as creme rinse, conditioner, body-adding lotions, etc. But that shelf will be well paid for in the increased ease and effectiveness in hair handling. The compliments you may get will be nice; but the greatest benefit will come as people see that being a Christian does *not* mean having limp, stringy hair and a bedraggled look.

By the time you reach this point in the chapter, some of you may be thinking, "I'm a housewife with three kids and a hectic schedule!" The overwhelming majority of us can say basically the same thing. But how does that busy housewife status rule out paying attention to the picture we present each day to husband, children, neighbors and acquaintances?

It needn't take you *long* to make yourself look presentable first thing in the morning. As stewards of the Lord's time and holders of domestic responsibilities, we should have our make-up/hair routine down to a 10-20 minute time slot from start to finish. But those minutes *are* important! They're important to the eyes of our family members because of the message they convey concerning our caring or not caring enough about those we love to look good for them. They are also important to our own eyes: seeing a pale, worn-out-looking self in the mirror lowers our spirits a notch or two—and

lowered spirits lower our quality of and joyful-
ness in our daily living.

For you who are married, just consider one
of your daily "contacts"—your husband. Was
the fine print on your marriage certificate a
license to disintegrate in your appearance?
Rather than letting marriage (whether 25
months or 25 years long) be an excuse against
maintaining a good appearance, it should be
your strongest motivation *for* that effort! The
greatest compliment a woman can pay a man is
keeping herself attractive for him. So let's go on
with a few final thoughts.

What about following the fashion trends in
hair? You know, one season curly is "in"; the
next, it's nothing but ruler-straight locks
wherever you look; short or long; pouffed or
flat. Applying the principle of balance which is so
important in the Christian life, stick to a general
outline which is best for your face, body proportions, and features; within that outline, have the
imaginative flexibility to adapt your hair style so
that it has just a hint of what's current. A case in
point has been the hold-on-to-the-death attitude of Christian women with bouffant hair
styles. All that back-combing and high-piling
was so hopelessly outmoded by the blow-dry
and curling-iron era that those who clung to it
made spectacles of themselves. It is *not* wise to
gallop along trying to keep up with every little
spurt of fashion—but neither is it wise to be so
far out in left field with a years-gone-by hairdo
that those seeing you react with "Ohhh,

brother!!" or "Yuck!"

Finally, there is one aspect of hair that is uniquely a concern of Christian women: its *length*. Some believers feel very strongly that hair should be long. Indeed, the Bible speaks of a woman's hair as her "crown," her "covering." As to the question, "What *is* long," we can know surely that any haircut so short it looks mannish violates the bounds set by God's Word. In today's society, hair is classified as long if it passes the mid-point of the neck. Some Christians feel that only waist- or hip-length hair can suffice as "long." A genuine conviction in this matter is certainly to be honored. At the same time, however, we need to be sure that "conviction" is not a convenient cover term for legalism, self-righteousness, or pride. I have known many girls and women whose flowing tresses in no way offset their frozen charity!

Regardless of hair's length, it is incumbent upon a woman claiming to represent the Lord to wear her hair *attractively* and *appropriately*. The attractive aspect has already been covered in preceding pages. Appropriateness has to do with two things: occasion and age.

If you can style your hair attractively in several different ways, the one you choose to wear at a particular time should be determined by the nature of your activity at that time. While working as a secretary, or attending school, for example, your hair should have a smooth, neat, un-fussy appearance: either loose-flowing or fussily-styled hair is inappropriate to such pursuits. Evening social occasions, on the other hand, provide an opportunity for the "extra pains" hair styles we enjoy now and then.

Appropriateness has to do, also, with age. A fourteen-year-old looks ridiculous in a sophisticated style designed for a mature woman, and grandmothers are *not* cute in ponytails or waist-length manes! Styling should be suitable to our years.

Personal Pinpointing

1. I can honestly say that I have accepted my face—every feature—as the one God pre-planned and created as *just right* for me. By His grace, I will not complain about, belittle, or take pride in the way I look.

(Signed) _____

2. My facial shape is most nearly _____ .

3. My most attractive facial feature is _____ .

4. My _____ can be made more attractive in appearance by _____ .

5. According to this chapter, I need to change the way I've been handling eyebrow pencil and/or mascara by _____ .

6. My present hairstyle is (right/wrong) for my facial shape and physical proportions.

7. In doing the "carpet comparison" test (see this chapter's **Spiritual Balance** page), I've discovered that _____

_____.

I'm going to determine to_____

_____.

Spiritual Balance

Now that we have examined our faces and hair styles, we need to do an even more careful study of something else: our carpet. Carpet? Right. The desire of the Christian woman should be *total loveliness*. Powder and paint cannot long hide a shallow brain or a sickly soul. So—examine your carpet. Where does it show greater wear: where you pray, or where you preen? Rightly, of course, it should be the former. If not, that's where the most earnest corrective measures need to be taken! If your spiritual life is anemic, flabby, unlovely, the mirror you need to use more is that of God's Word. "Beauty is only skin deep" should never be truthfully applied to a born-again Christian woman. Not a single day should pass when we don't spend time beautifying our souls through Bible study, memorization, and prayer.

4

Grace: –ful or –less

Are you finished enhancing your loveliness for the Lord's sake when you've carefully attended to face and hair? Not by a long shot, though you might judge otherwise by the bearing of many women. Posture and carriage deposit to or withdraw from our appearance accounts.

Excluding professionally-oriented training classes and special "finishing" schools, emphasis upon graceful carriage is almost non-existent. This lack is sadly evident everywhere; its results, though, are especially regrettable in Christian women. Why? Because of all women, we who know Christ as Saviour should be exemplary in our physical bearing, that we might more clearly reflect the Creator's original design. His plan was that we should be *upright* in posture and carriage—but as we have departed spiritually from His intention, so too have we departed physically.

There are several spiritually-oriented reasons for a born-again girl or woman to excel in posture and carriage:

1. **You are a daughter of the King of Glory.** As that wonderful truth makes your heart stand tall with gratitude, so it should make your body illustrate the internal uprightness.

2. **You are to serve as a magnet and mirror for your Lord.** The distinctive *difference* of an erect, gracefully feminine carriage from contemporary slumping and slinking will of itself be a testimony.

3. **You should seek to fulfill your Lord's intention for femininity.** The more the world screams "Unisex!" by dress, carriage, and actions, the more clearly do you need to reject and contradict that ungodly emphasis in each of those areas. A graceful, womanly posture and carriage is a silent statement that you reject the world's philosophy.

4. **You must, as God's child, obey His command for modesty.** Knowledge and practice in proper carriage will help you immeasurably in this important aspect.

5. **The Holy Spirit's indwelling of your body as His temple makes it imperative that you take the best possible care of it.** Good posture is a positive factor in good health. You will have more energy and will be less tired if you carry yourself correctly. You may also prevent menstrual cramps, backache, and even headaches by correcting poor posture.

Having, then, established the rationale for

this study of posture and carriage, let's move on to its discussion.

STANDING

Good posture is basically *upright stance*. Look at a toddler's posture. It's beautiful! The little back is straight, the chest high, the head erect. But as the child grows, he learns by example to "crumple" in his posture. Very soon, poor posture becomes habitual with him.

There are several basic postural distortions:

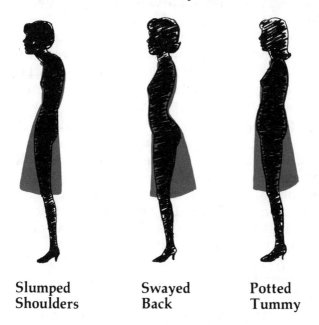

| **Slumped** | **Swayed** | **Potted** |
| **Shoulders** | **Back** | **Tummy** |

Sketches are one thing, but reality is infinitely better (worse?). Stand so you can see your side view in a full-length mirror. Which one of the poor postures sketched does your *habitual* stance most closely resemble? (Don't cheat and "pull up" for this analytical look!) Awful? Well, then, grit your teeth, ask for the Lord's help, and set out to replace bad habits with good ones!

The key to good posture is proper body alignment. When you are standing correctly, an imaginary line could be drawn the length of your body's side view. Study the facing page for how to bring your body into proper alignment. Do you feel uncomfortable when you've pulled your body into this proper alignment? Don't be discouraged. After all, the longer you've practiced poor posture, the harder it will be to break your bad habits. But the improvement, not only in the way you look but also in the way you feel, will make your efforts more than worthwhile.

By *posture alone* a woman can make a $200 dress look like a grab-bag reject. Conversely, erect carriage can make a $2 bargain look expensive. To convince yourself of this fact, put any one of your outfits on a dress form adjusted to your measurements. Notice how attractively the dress fits and hangs. Now put it on your *own* form, and assume your habitual posture. See how you alter the whole visual effect? Makes you wonder which one is the dummy, doesn't it?

Correcting poor posture habits will take long, hard work; it will mean checking up on your body alignment every little while all through the day every day: when any one

Head
chin parallel to the
floor (neither raised;
"snooty" nor lowered:
"defeated") ears riding
directly over shoulders

Neck
upright, a straight
column rising from the
shoulders; neither
thrust forward or
craned backward

Chest
lifted out of belt line

Tummy
pulled in absolutely
flat. (Here, you may
have really let your
muscles "go to pot"!
Don't let them stay
there. Retrain and keep
them in tone. Just a
pulled-in tummy takes
pounds off your
appearance!)

Shoulders
back and down, re-
laxed rather than stiff
(not "military"). To
find proper position:
with rib cage high,
raise shoulders as far
toward the ears as
possible, then let them
relax into a down-and-
back position.

Back
straight and tall, hav-
ing only a *very* slight
natural curve at waist

Derriere
the pelvis (bony girdle
onto which your legs
are hinged) should be
tipped so the rear is
tucked somewhat un-
der. (This lops off the
"back porch" look.)

Knees
slightly flexed

Feet
weight evenly dis-
tributed between balls
and heels. Feet should
be parallel to each
other—neither point-
ed out nor in.

section regresses into its unlovely old ways, you will have to pull it back into proper alignment right away. The desired goal is consistently good posture—not just a "know-how-to-but-only-use-on-special-occasions" type. The harder, more faithfully you work to overcome poor habits, the sooner they'll be replaced by good ones. Oh—and don't let tiredness be an excuse. In fact, the more tired you are, the more important good posture is! Case in point: pick a time when you feel you've expended every ounce of energy; now pull up into your tallest, straightest posture, take the time to draw several long, full breaths into your newly-uncramped lungs, and feel how some of the exhaustion immediately lifts. Multiply that effect by consistent proper bearing throughout the day, and you've provided for yourself a generous boost toward increased physical energy and efficiency.

WALKING

Actually, walking is not a separate consideration, for proper carriage is simply good posture *in action*. Additional considerations for movement are few and simple.

First, the body should appear unified in its walking: smooth, coordinated, and graceful. Your best private teacher for this aspect of your training would be a candid moving picture film of your habitual walk. You'd be quick to see jerkiness, turkey-head movement, and many other characteristics of poor carriage. If that kind of celluloid tutor is out of the question, observe yourself in some plate glass windows for the side view and in your own full-length mirror for the front and rear views.

The only parts of your body that should show any appreciable movement in walking are your legs and arms. Head and shoulders should remain still! Arms swing naturally at the sides—slightly curved and relaxed rather than stiff and militaristic. They move in opposition to the legs: when the right leg is forward, the left arm is forward, and vice versa.

As for the legs themselves, the walking movement ideally comes from the thighs down—there is no necessity for extraneous hip-swinging. The idea is to swing *from* the hips—not to swing the hips themselves. A woman naturally has a bit more movement in the hip area than does a man, due to physical structure; but a pronounced, attention-getting, "movie star" swish of the hips should be *out* for a born-again woman! Such a walk is so closely associated with the "Come on, boys!" worldly emphasis that a woman must be very careful to avoid it.

Second, the feet should be placed just to either side of an imaginary line. If you try to walk *on* that line, you will look teeter-y. But keeping the inner side of each foot skimming the line will keep you from walking with a wide-track, ungainly gait.

Third, toes must remain parallel to each other throughout the walk. Toes pointing either out or in detract greatly from an aura of gracefulness.

Fourth, your stride should be about the length of your shoe: that will keep you from the too-long stride of a furrow-crossing fieldhand or the too-short steps of a Mincing Minerva.

Fifth, weight is constantly, smoothly shifted during walking. As you step forward, weight comes down first on the heel of the forward foot (but don't wham all your weight down like a lumberjack!), moves smoothly onto the middle and ball of the foot, then springs forward off the toes as the other leg comes forward.

What about carrying a purse? The type with a moderate-sized handle or strap is more gracefully carried over your arm, with the arm coming *from the outside in* through the strap. A small-handled bag, a clutch, or an envelope type purse may be carried in your hand in the extended, normal standing/walking position, or under your arm just above the elbow. A shoulder bag, of course, should live up to its design when you carry it.

PIVOTING

The pivot may be an item of graceful movement you've not considered, but adding it to your store of "moving knowledge" will contribute a happy "plus" to your carriage.

A pivot is simply a turn: the most efficient and graceful method of turning. Practice the following description and diagram until the pivot becomes second nature to you:

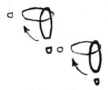

(This is a pivot to the right.)

1. At the end of a line of walking, "close" with the rear (right, in this instance) foot—that is, bring the right toe forward until it is approximately on a plane with the left instep.

2. Shift weight onto the balls of the feet.

3. Lifting the heels of both feet slightly off the floor, turn to the right without lifting balls of feet from floor at all. Return heels to floor, and you're ready to move off at a right angle from your original line of walking.

4. In pivoting all the way around to go back in the direction from which you came, there will have to be an imperceptible lifting/sliding of the right foot as you pivot. The pivot technique is not really difficult; but if you find, after a fair number of attempts that it feels "stilted" to you, by all means, forget it! You should never try to look like a self-conscious, posing clothing model. The ideal is to practice the pivot *until it becomes the natural way for you to turn.*

SITTING

A simple chair can be a big enemy to gracefulness. The challenge, however, is conquerable.

Many women recognize the enmity of chairs but capitulate and crumple into the sitting position in hopes that speed will camouflage awkwardness. Empty hopes! *Graceful control* is the key for proper sitting.

Avoid the ungainly practices of:

Craning backwards to keep an eye on the chair (It's not going to walk away!)

Slinging your spine into a C-curve, forcing your derriere into a yards-ahead lead.

Plopping your weight down onto the chair as if dropped from a steeple.

Practice the following steps for graceful sitting until the entire movement is easy and natural for you:

Look at the chair as you approach it—check for position and height.

Stop looking at the chair; pivot gracefully in front of it.

With your back to the chair, position one leg so your calf touches the seat front. This provides a physical re-check of position and height.

Keeping your *back straight*, your *head erect*, lower yourself *in one smooth movement* into the chair. Your thigh muscles should do almost all the work; don't let them go off duty until you are satisfactorily seated. (If you discover that your thigh muscles have grown weak, incorporate daily deep-knee bends to whip them back into shape.)

Allow your arms to hang at your sides as you sit; your hands can be unobtrusively straightening your skirt on your way down. (Don't grab the chair arms and heave yourself into position!)

Once seated, as nearly as possible keep your body in a slight S-curve. Don't yank at your skirt, wriggle, twist, or otherwise make a production of finding a comfortable position.

Hands may rest in your lap or on the chair arms.

Keep your back and head erect, and sit on the *bottom* of your spine—not the middle or top of it!

Cross legs at ankles rather than at knees. (Suggested by doctors, too, by the way!)

Finally, and this is a cardinal rule, *keep knees and ankles together*! Don't be a Graceless Grangelmina.

SPECIAL CHALLENGES TO GRACE

There are a few actions that can make us feel particularly like ice-bound cows:

Putting on or removing a coat

(with help)

—*Avoid* backing and flapping like a retreating hen.

—Approach the coat face forward as it's held by your escort, visually checking its height.

—Put one arm into a sleeve.

—Pivot toward that arm.

—Bring other arm around behind you to the height of the lead arm, find armhole, and slip arm into it.

—Allow escort to lift coat onto your shoulders.

—Remove by reversing above actions.

(without help)

—Place one arm in coat, raise coat partially onto that arm and shoulder.

—Reach around back with the other arm and place it in second coat sleeve.

—Pull coat up onto shoulders by both hands drawing lapels upward.

—Remove by dropping coat off one shoulder, allowing it to slide off that arm. Bring free arm around in front, grasp shoulder seam near collar as it slides off second arm. Place shoulder seams together, and hang, folded, across one arm if you're not planning to put coat on a hanger.

Although any description is necessarily disjoint-ed, the actions can actually be molded into one smooth, fluid movement.

Entering and exiting a car

—Sit first (unless the car is VERY little and low, or if entering the back seat of a two-door).

—Swing legs up and in, in one smooth movement, *keeping knees and ankles together.*

—Exit by reversing the described move-ment. (The "exception" situations mentioned above can best be tackled by a step-forward-while-crouching technique. Understandably, such a maneuver won't win any awards for gracefulness.)

Sitting on table-attached picnic benches

—Set your food-laden plate down on the table.

—Step over the bench, one leg at a time, in the standing position.

—OR—

—Sit on bench with back toward the table; gather skirt closely around knees; swing both legs over simultaneously, *keeping knees and ankles together.*

Picking up an object from floor or ground

—Do NOT bend from waist and hips, making yourself look like a stinkbug.

—DO keep back straight; bend at the knees. Go into a deep knee bend, using your thigh muscles to power the movement.

In the preceding few pages we have covered the basic principles for good posture and carriage. If the principles merely remain black squiggles on white sheets of paper, they won't do you an iota of good. But if you will transfer them to your mind and translate them into consistent practice in your body, you will demonstrate the kind of feminine grace which states your delight in the Lord's crowning creation—womanhood.

Personal Pinpointing

1. My posture check-up shows that I need to overcome _____

_____ .

2. My carriage can be helped by the following improvements: _____

_____

3. The most difficult thing for me to remember in sitting gracefully is: _____

_____ .

4. Watching my feet, I see that they _____

when I walk. That means I (do/don't) need to break some placement habits.

5. The toughest "challenge to grace" for me in this chapter is _____

_____ , because _____

_____ .

Spiritual Balance

While considering your posture and carriage physically, realize that of far greater import is the uprightness of your inner woman. Do your ethics stand tall? Do you stoop to petty gossip? Do you slump into small deceits? Do you have a swaybacked character which "adjusts" to please whatever crowd you're with at a given moment? And what of your spiritual movement—is it *forward* for and toward the Lord? Do your soul's feet walk upon the distinctly-drawn line of His Holy Word? If the inner woman is not characterized by God's grace reflected, any physical grace is wasted.

5

The Significant Silhouette

When you and your friends get together for casual conversation, how long does it take for someone to bring up the topic of weight? Probably not very long. Almost all women, regardless of age or occupation, are interested in weight—whether it be for gaining, shifting, losing, or maintaining.

When we discuss weight, we're not talking about what our skeletal framework does to the scale needle, but about what our fleshy outline does to it. And what variety there is in fleshy outlines!

Why do you have a constant battle against weight while your best friend never needs to give it a thought, and your sister has to drink milkshakes at night to maintain her weight? The basic determining factors are bone structure, body type, and metabolic rate.

Bone structure is divided into three categories: small, medium, and large. A tall, large-boned woman should not expect to weigh the same as a tall, small-boned woman. Her bones *alone* weigh more. And because the bones are larger, it takes more "meat" to cover them.

Body type, too, has three divisions: endomorphic, ectomorphic, and mesomorphic. The endomorphic is that type which tends to weightiness, while the ectomorphic is naturally slender; the mesomorphic is muscular and athletic. Recognizing the existence and characteristics of these physical types can help you complete your query, "Why do I . . . ?" with regard to weight.

And finally, your metabolic rate has an influence on your weight. That is, the efficiency with which you assimilate and utilize your food. In this aspect, too, there is great variation: hence your highly energetic, thin-as-a-rail sister versus your more sluggish, weight-tending self.

It can help your mental/emotional outlook to know which type you most nearly represent in all three weight-determining factors. Having done that, decide (realistically and honestly) what your best weight is. Unless you have been overweight since childhood, your weight at about age eighteen will probably have been ideal. For those of you who are younger than eighteen, the height/weight charts available through various insurance companies and medical offices are generally applicable. Whatever your age, it's important that you don't just snatch a weight out of mid-air as your ideal: it may be quite impractical. And you certainly should not choose your perfect weight on the basis of what some friend weighs!

Abundant food and sedentary living have seen to it that our major weight concern in America has to do with *over*weight. Because so many have problems controlling their weight, and because overweight can have an adverse effect upon Christian testimony, some serious thinking is in order.

First of all, in considering the variables determining weight, be sure that you don't use any of them as an excuse for obvious over-weight. Likewise, in by far the major number of instances, the "glandular problems" often claimed as excuses are really *gluttony* problems.

Obesity could well be called the "ignored" or "forgotten" sin among Bible-believing Christians—but no matter how consistently it may be overlooked from (and in) the pulpit, it is no less a sin!

Food, of course, is intended as the fuel for our bodies. When our food intake outstrips our physical demands, it builds excess fat. And medical studies show that every pound of extra fat works against peak efficiency and health of the body. So, despite our efforts to equivocate, we *put on* weight because we *put in* too much food.

Scripture is surely and unshakably against overeating, calling it "gluttony." Passages such as the following are applicable:

Be not among winebibbers, among riotous

> (gluttonous) eaters of flesh: For the
> drunkard and the glutton shall come to
> poverty: and drowsiness shall clothe a
> man with rags.   (Proverbs 23:20, 21)

(Evidently gluttony should be kept out of our
lives even by association!)

God's warnings against self-indulgence do
not stop with its effect upon externals—they are
issued with an eye to spiritual implications:

> And every man that striveth for the
> mastery is temperate in all things.
> (I Corinthians 9:25a)
>
> But I keep under my body, and bring it
> into subjection.   (I Corinthians 9:27a)
>
> He that hath no rule over his own spirit is
> like a city that is broken down, and with-
> out walls.   (Proverbs 25:28)

Because overeating is a manifestation of
weak self-discipline and pandering to fleshly
desires, it can have an unwholesome effect upon
the testimony God wants us to bear for Him.

Our bodies are declared to be the tabernacles wherein the Holy Spirit, third Person of the
Trinity, graciously comes to dwell when a
person accepts Jesus Christ as personal Saviour
(I Corinthians 6:19, 20). How we dishonor Him
by mistreating His tabernacle in *any* way—
including loading it with fat!

Listening to a young woman give her testimony concerning her weight loss of nearly one
hundred pounds and her increased usefulness to
the Lord thereby, I was particularly impressed to

hear her tell how conviction had taken hold of her when, before meals, she would bow her head and pray, "Bless this food to my body." That phrase cut to her heart because she realized the incongruity of asking the Lord to bless her sin of gluttony! Standing slim and radiant on the platform, this girl went on to say, "I was *miserable* when I was fat! I was ashamed of my weakness, ashamed of my weight: I hated me. I knew that my fat was a terrible testimony to the elementary school children I taught. I wouldn't go back to that misery for anything!"

"But," you may wail, "You don't understand *why* I overeat!" By that, you're referring to some emotional or psychological motivation behind your food-intake problem. You may point to one or more of the following:

"I'm lonely."

"My husband isn't what he ought to be."

"My circumstances of life are *awful*."

"I'm worried."

"My life is full of insecurities."

"Nobody loves me."

I wouldn't discount for a moment the reality and severity of such problems. But wait a minute. *Does stuffing really help*? If you're honest, you'll have to admit that it does not. In fact, it makes matters worse—because eating orgies add guilt feelings on top of the original problem, right? My dear lady friend, it's useless to seek solutions/compensations in food. Instead, the correction of the problems lies in giving them to the Lord. ("Casting *all* your care upon him; for he careth for you" I Peter 5:7.) The greater the problem, the more constant must be the casting. We throw our burdens upon our burden-bearing Lord by talking to Him in prayer and by letting Him talk to us through His Word.

If at this point the Holy Spirit is convicting you of the sin of gluttony, prompting you toward weight loss for the sake of your health, your character, and your testimony, can you expect the Lord to make the fat melt? No. You got it on—you're going to have to get it off! The hard fact is, every excess pound we carry can only be dropped via the rigors of appetite adjustment and intake control: *dieting*.

There are as many weight-loss diets around today as anyone could possibly wish. Rather than recommending any one over another, I would urge you to find one that best fits your individual manner of life and your pocketbook. Beyond that, here are just a few suggestions which may be applied to whatever diet program you undertake.

In looking back to numberless diets you may have already tried, stop saying "They failed," and admit "*I* failed." The diet is only an inanimate *thing*. Full responsibility for success or failure rests squarely upon the dieter.

See your doctor for a thorough physical examination before starting on any diet plan. Confirm the ideal weight you want to reach, and have him suggest the severity/length/type diet you should follow.

Make up your mind that you *will* succeed on

this weight-loss project. Then pray about it: confess your gluttony as a sin against the Lord Himself and against the tabernacle of His Holy Spirit. Plead His forgiveness and claim His empowering for success. That prayer for strength is going to have to be repeated over and over again throughout the days of your dieting.

Unless you join a weight-loss organization, make the Lord the *only* one you talk to about your diet! Keep it a matter of covenant between the two of you. The effective dieter is one who doesn't talk about her eating regime—she uses all her energy to stick to it!

Change your attitudes about eating. Form the habit of giving yourself a cross-examination concerning every temptation to eat, something like this:

Q: Why do I want to eat at this moment?

A: I'm lonely.

Q: What real help can eating afford to my loneliness?

A: None.

Q: What *can* I do to ease the emptiness?

A: Stop thinking about my emotions or my "hunger" and get up and do something active— preferably something for somebody else. (NOTE: No matter how pathetic you as questioner may sound in any instance of temptation, be sure that you as answerer are coldly, unmovingly honest and blunt.)

Don't weigh every day. That's a good way to grow discouraged. Instead, get on the scales only once or twice a week.

Replace old eating habits and preferences with *permanent* new ones. Just because you're used to taking three helpings of everything doesn't mean you *always* must take three helpings! Make a "no seconds" rule such an overriding control that anything else becomes unthinkable. Learn to really like fresh vegetables and fruits instead of sauces, gravies, etc.

For a gnawing sweet tooth, fool your taste buds—eat a lemon or a pickle.

Remove the "food traps" that have heretofore wreaked havoc on your diet attempts. If, for example, TV-watching automatically gets your gastric juices screaming for snacks, cut out TV. You'll reap a double benefit: removal of non-edifying material for your soul and non-essential calories for your body. Replace the sit-and-chomp TV habit with a hands-busy-mind-working habit. For example, work on a latch-hook rug while listening to Scripture, sermon, or sacred music tapes. You'll do some inward growing *and* some outward shrinking!

Be satisfied with slow but steady weight loss. "Crash" diets are unwise and unsafe. Weight that comes off quickly also comes back on quickly. Realize, too, that you will occasionally hit "plateaus" where your weight will hold steady for several weeks. *Don't throw the diet out the window*! Stick with it—eventually your body will adjust downward, and you'll begin losing again.

Adjust your thinking from "get it off" to "keep it off." In order to do that, most of us have to accept the fact that *for the rest of our lives* we'll have to watch our scales and our silhouettes carefully. A good rule, scale-wise, is to never let yourself gain over two pounds once you've trimmed down to your ideal weight. When the needle on the indicator touches that two-pound limit, cut back immediately on your food intake. Don't be tolerant with yourself!

Be sure to incorporate appropriate excerise into any weight-loss/maintenance plan. Dieting can leave you flabby. Exercise eliminates flab internally as well as externally. Moreover, it's a boon for your cardiovascular system and it works to help curb and re-direct your appetite. Don't consider excercise a "maybe" part of your diet, but a "must."

Beyond the practical aids prescribed above, the born-again woman can claim the spiritual aids of Scripture:

> Set a watch, O Lord, before my mouth;
> keep the door of my lips. Incline not my
> heart to any evil thing, to practice wicked
> works with men that work iniquity: and
> let me not eat of their dainties.
>
> (Psalm 141:3,4)

> Not that we are sufficient of ourselves to
> think anything as of ourselves; but our
> sufficiency is of God.
>
> (II Corinthians 3:5)

Anyone who has ever tried to lose a pound can tell you that it's no snap! Dieting means hunger pangs, unsatisfied cravings, and an occasional twinge of self-pity when you're sitting next to Naturally-Willowy Willa while she devours six rolls dripping with butter. But weight loss and control also mean some tremendous pluses for a Christian woman:

+ for your energy and endurance
+ for your character growth through self-discipline
+ for your testimony before unsaved and saved alike

Diet may seem a very small battlefield in thinking of the great spiritual warfare in which we believers are engaged. Nevertheless, it *is* a field of encounter with our Adversary (it's certainly not the *Lord* who whispers, "Oh, go on—indulge yourself in those unnecessary calories!"); all too often, the encounter becomes a Waterloo. What we learn by enduring hardness in a "little thing" like diet can be used of the Lord to strengthen us for the greater spiritual battlegrounds that lie ahead. And through moment-by-moment strengthening by our Saviour we *can* gain, claim, and keep the land formerly held by self and the devil.

Personal Pinpointing

1. My bone structure is _____ .
               (small/medium/large)
2. My body type seems to be _____ .
   (endomorphic, ectomorphic, mesomorphic)

3. My ideal weight is _____ .

4. At this moment I am _____ .
(overweight/underweight/at my ideal weight)

5. If I need to diet to reach my ideal weight, my personal "cross-examination" when I get the urge to eat should go like this: (BE HONEST AND SPECIFIC!)

Q: _____ ?
A: _____ .
Q: _____ ?
A: _____ .
Q: _____ ?
A: _____ .
Q: _____ ?
A: _____ .

6. My worst "food trap" is _____ .

Spiritual Balance

As our physical concern with regard to weight should be *good health* and *good appearance*, so should our spiritual concern. A soul can grow lean to the point of emaciation if we feed it the "junk food" of feelings and rationalization. Or it can grow monstrously fat and sluggish from ingesting spiritual food but never exercising. Witnessing, teaching, discipling new converts, rendering physical and spiritual care for Christian sisters—these are the spiritual calisthentics we need in our daily schedule so that we can maintain a healthy, vigorous internal silhouette.

6

Closet Clues

Having dealt with the size and type of your physical frame, let's now consider what to put on that frame. We've already touched upon cleanliness and basic fit of garments. But what of style, coordination, and appropriateness?

Clothes don't *make* a woman, of course, but they certainly *mark* her. What does your clothing say about you?

It's typical of the feminine nature to be interested in clothing. Nor is clothes interest condemned by Scripture except as it gets *out of proportion* in our lives. Remember that the virtuous woman of Proverbs 31 is described as being dressed in "silk and purple." In other words, she's *very well dressed*!

Some women have considerably more innate "clothes savvy" than others; but every woman can learn some practical clothing guidelines and thereby work a world of improvement in her appearance.

A Christian woman should *not* try for a lead role in the Fashion Frantics. The extreme swings in fashion from season to season and year to year are a calculated effort of the garment industry to keep the buyer's pockets empty and the industry's coffers full. And women by the millions fall for the phony build-ups of "what's new" or "what's in"—a sad waste of energy, emphasis, and money! Fashion has reached the point where very few women really look good in the industry's trend setters. I, for one, greatly resent designers who evidently hate women, and manufacturers who play us for financial idiots! Instead of succumbing to the pressures and blandishments of the ever-changing fashion scene, a Christian woman needs to exercise wisdom and restraint—by recognizing her own personal style and adapting the elements of fashion to it. This is done by observing certain guidelines.

The *primary* consideration of a born-again woman must be modesty. Scripture demands it: therefore certain trends and garments will automatically be bypassed. At this point, a brief discussion of what constitutes modesty of fit is in order. The term "too tight" is often used, but apparently seldom understood.

The clothing of a redeemed woman must not give her the appearance of a reprobate woman by suggestively hugging body curves. This is a matter in which *masculine makeup* must be taken into account. In making mankind male and female, God saw fit to create the male with sexual instincts which are aroused by what he *sees*, while the woman is touch-oriented. Saved or unsaved, men are alike in this basic, instinctive aspect; the difference lies in their *reaction* to the stimulation of sight. The ungodly man seeks, revels in, and succumbs to it. The godly man, on the contrary, must curb and confine it. Our responsibility, therefore, as Christian women, is great: we must NOT dress in such a way as to promiscuously stimulate boys and men. The danger does not lie just in uncovering; in some ways, clothing which reveals *by suggestion* holds greater allure than that which reveals in fact.

Another principle basic to a Christian woman's entire appearance is *femininity*. It is vital to remember that "male and female created He them." The unsaved are dedicated to erasing or distorting the differences God created—but that "unisex" effort must be shunned by us who know the Lord through personal, saving faith.

Webster uses such words as "gentleness," "delicacy," and "modesty" to denote femininity; that which is feminine has a softness and sweetness about it. In clothing, that does *not* mean we have to wear ruffles and bows constantly; there are pursuits and occasions when frou-frous are inappropriate. It does mean, however, that we should consistently strive for "softening" in line or detailing and shun harshness, sloppiness, or mannishness. For example, you do well to choose tailored suits for business wear; but avoid carrying the tailored look into the realm of *severity*.

In a nutshell, we Christian women, while avoiding both immodesty and "sexiness," should express our delight in our God-given femininity by our appearance, attitude, and actions.

Specifically, then, here are some guidelines on modest fit of clothing:

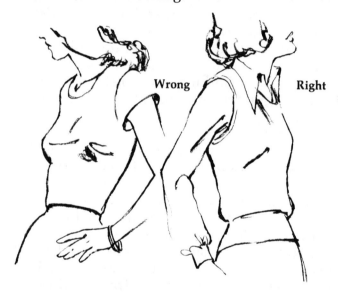

Wrong   Right

Bust. At least one inch of excess fullness in material at point of bustline.

No horizontal pulling of fabric.

No strain-caused placket gaps.

No "cupping under" of fabric to reveal outline of breasts. (Knits are infamous for this!)

No revelation of nipples by combination of thin-fabric bra plus clinging outerwear.

Hips. At least one inch of excess fullness in garment at broadest point of hips.

No horizontal pulling of fabric.

No "cupping under" of fabric to reveal hips.

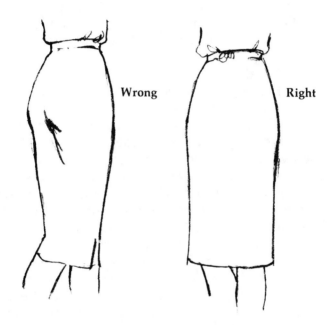

Wrong   Right

Miscellaneous: don't wear blouses or bodices with sleeves so deep-cut or wide-cut that movement of your arms makes it possible to see into the garment.

Avoid clinging fabrics anywhere on the body. For example, a woman or girl looks decidedly un-cute (even from the back!) when a garment reveals her above-or-below-the-bra lumpiness.

OF SPECIAL NOTE: The standard of modesty with regard to fit at the hips which has just been described and illustrated applies to dresses, skirts, slacks, and culottes! (Culottes also present another problem: their wide-cut legs make modesty very difficult—not only in strenuous activities, but also in sitting.)

Second, determine your individual life style by taking the following factors into account:
—Region
—Locale
—Focus of endeavor
—Social activities

Let's discuss those influencing factors.

Region: the section of the nation in which you live should have a bearing upon the way you dress. Basic climate varies from region to region, making a wardrobe which is suitable to the Northeast out of keeping to the Southwest. Likewise, the formality of life varies: the East is generally more formal in its clothing than is the West. The woman who wears spike heels, silk dresses, and big floppy hats in an area where sensible shoes, tailored daywear, and bare heads are the order of life calls undue attention (and resentment) to herself.

Locale: is it urban, suburban, or rural? Clothing worn in a farming community is likely to reflect comfort and practicality, while that worn in a large city leans toward sleekness and sophistication.

Focus of endeavor: upon what does your life center? School? Home care and child rearing? A business or professional career? Differences in life emphasis create differences in wardrobe needs.

Social activities: their range and frequency will play a part in your clothing choice. In other words, if you often attend luncheons, teas, and receptions, the dressier end of your closet needs to be more extensive than if your social activities consist of a yearly family reunion.

Third, consider your individuality. In spite of the fact that all of us have two arms, two legs, one head, a waist, shoulders, etc., the size and arrangement of those components results in endless variations. What looks good on one body may spell disaster on another. For example, ruffles and flounces are more suitable to a small-boned, slender form than to a large-boned, heavy-set one; but the latter may look smashing in a bold plaid which would overpower the smaller woman. Your personality is likewise unique. A bubbling type is better served by boldness in color and style, while a gentler type more accurately projects her personality with muted colors and conservative styling. It's important to remember that those models posturing and pouting from the magazine pages are simply human mannikins—there is no more reason to copy their outfits detail-by-detail than there is to copy their ridiculous poses!

Fourth, consider your figure. Never buy or make a piece of clothing because it looks good on a plastic dummy. Most of us are neither under-nourished fashion models nor the fabled 36-25-36. To dress as if we had a model's figure is only going to result in making us look ludicrous. Wisdom in this particular consideration lies in recognizing that we can dress *cosmetically*. This is done by applying principles of proportion, color, and line.

The proportionate size of prints, plaids, stripes, trims, and accessories should be neither overpowering nor miniaturized in comparison with your physique. Following are just a few illustrations of this principle:

Overweight Orbellina

Orbie should have avoided the big print and large collar in this dress. They accent her too-generous physical proportions. Her hat and bag, on the other hand, also call attention to her size because they are disproportionately small.

Tall Talmira

Talmira should not have chosen vertical stripes for her outfit. They draw the eye of the observer up—up—and up, accenting rather than minimizing her height.

Hippy Hepsiba

Hepsiba's large-plaid skirt makes her oversized hips look even larger. Also, the gathered style adds bulk right where she least needs it.

Busty Buzzelda

Buzzelda has accented her disproportionate figure (1) by wearing a light-colored top and (2) by wearing an attention-drawing contrast trim at the bustline.

Color can either emphasize or minimize, and it should be used accordingly. The principle to remember is that bright and light colors advance or enlarge, while deep and dark colors retreat or minimize. In other words, on your own figure you would "shrink" the apparent size of an over-large area by using deep colors there, keeping lighter tones where your proportions can afford some "expansion." The small-busted, narrow-shouldered woman, for example, does well to wear lighter, brighter tops with deep or dark skirts.

Besides proportion and color, line is an important consideration in clothing. Line directs the eye of the beholder. Look back at Talmira for an illustration of this principle. Learn to use line as a cosmetic tool in your wardrobe:

Horizontals—cut, emphasize, or broaden
Verticals—elongate, slim
Diagonals—slim

For example, look what a difference the change of *line only* makes on the same figure:

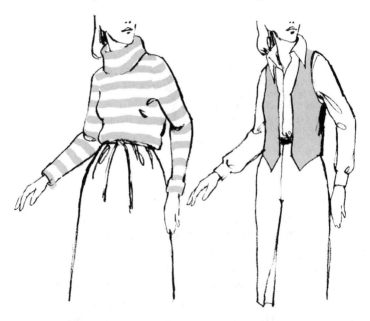

Don't forget that the waist seam of a garment is a line: use it to advantage. Your particular figure may be enhanced by either a raised or dropped waistline. For instance, a tall woman can minimize her height by wearing a dropped waistline. (The distance from feet to waist serves as a gauge for our visual judgment of height/length.) A dropped waistline will also help disguise a short-waisted figure. Conversely, a short woman can give the illusion of height by wearing an empire line.

BUILDING A WARDROBE

When you stand at your open closet door and groan, "I haven't a thing to wear," you're really saying, "I don't have anything appropriate for this occasion," or "I've nothing that goes with anything else." How does a woman prevent such a frustrating situation? By patiently but persistently *engineering* a wardrobe, applying the mechanics of proportion, color, line, and individuality and using the building blocks of coordination.

Does an "engineered" wardrobe mean (a) that you throw out everything you now have, (b) spend endless hours shopping from one end of town to the other, and (c) increase your financial outlay for clothing? It means none of those things. It *does* mean that you (a) get a firm mental grasp on the principles of wise clothing choice, forgetting old mental and purchasing/sewing habits that have put wasted clothing in your closet, (b) eliminate the "duds" through the gradual, normal cycle of wardrobe renewal, (c) always keep a list of needed clothing items, colors, and types in your purse in the event you stumble on a great sale (which without the reminder of your list could send you into ecstasies of impulse—but unwise—buying), and (d) actually SAVE your money.

Now, let's go on to consider the "building blocks" of coordination. They will save your patience and your pocketbook while simultaneously expanding your wardrobe's practicality.

Coordination is basically a matter of *color*. The color of your outfit determines the color of your accessories—scarf, shoes, bag, hat, gloves, etc. We get ourselves into some royal messes by pulling a *brown* dress from the closet only to realize that none but our *navy* shoes are fit to wear, and only the red purse has an unbroken handle! Buying, storing, and wearing clothing is greatly simplified by *color-keying* a wardrobe.

The first step is to decide on *one* basic color for winter clothing, another for summer wear. The best winter basics are:

Black

Brown

Navy

Best summer basics consist of only two:

Cream

White

Your choice of basic color is decided by which one is best for your particular hair/complexion/eyes combination. *There is one* which does far more for you than the others, by flattering your skin tones rather than giving a sallow or colorless cast and by heightening the effect of eyes and hair. If you have trouble deciding which is most flattering to you, enlist the aid of a relative or friend who has an "artistic" eye and sound judgment.

Foundational to your wardrobe will be the following:

1 pair everyday plain pumps

1 pair dressy pumps (or buy the plains only, plus a fancy buckle for dressier occasions)

1 basic purse

1 basic dress

1 basic skirt

1 basic suit

1 basic coat

1 contrast or complement blouse

The word "basic" used repeatedly in the listing above refers not only to the garment's color, but also to the style: classic simplicity with any trim, buttons, belt, and detailing *in the basic color*. If you're accustomed to buying or making clothes in a helter-skelter manner, this "basic" approach may at first seem pretty "blah." But wait a minute. This is your *foundation* closet-wise. As such, the simpler the clothing the better: the usefulness of the garments is automatically expanded thereby. That is, the garment serves somewhat like an empty artist's canvas upon which you may "paint" varying degrees of formality or informality. Your "artist's brush" will apply such things as scarves, necklaces, pins, collars, cuffs, weskits, jackets, etc.

Establish the color-keyed wardrobe foundation as suggested both in your summer and in your winter wear. From this starting point, *all* your buying or sewing should be done in patterns, fabrics, and colors that *coordinate with* your foundational unit. That guideline will eliminate the kind of impulse buying that adds another outfit to your closet but makes it necessary to buy "something to go with it."

As time and finances make it possible, you may well want to expand out of your fundamental color scheme. But add one color or color family at a time, and coordinate carefully around that new color.

CLOTHES CLUES

As you add coordinating colors and pieces to your closet, aim for *quality* and *simplicity*. Together, they will stretch your dollar and your clothing's usefulness.

In apparel, as in other things, you definitely get what you pay for! Therefore it's important that you school yourself in recognizing quality— not just in makers' names, but also in construction and fabric details. Just a few hallmarks of quality to look for are:

Generous, non-puckering, even hemline.

Full or partial (at *least* in seat) lining in wools.

Non-pouching darts; bust darts hitting accurately for *your* figure: level with the fullest point.

Sturdily-sewn, generous seams (bound edges on ravel-y fabrics).

Pockets and collars sewn without ripples.

Plaids and stripes matching at the seams.

Neat appearance to finish work inside garment.

Quality "feel" in fabric.

Be a wise shopper: haunt sales, outlet stores, and re-sale shops. Avoid impulse buying: remember, nothing's a bargain if you don't need it!

Now and then all of us face moments when we wonder, "What should I wear for this occasion?" Those are the moments when knowledge of a few basic dressing principles pays big dividends in assurance and appropriateness. Let's consider some of those principles.

First of all, we need to recognize the fact that *simplicity* is the key to tasteful appearance. (A very helpful rule to be applied also in determining how much jewelry to wear with any given outfit, by the way. Hold it to the *minimum*.)

"Safety" of appearance lies in wearing two or three colors in an outfit—four gives an overdone or helter-skelter look.

Shoes should always be as dark as or darker than the outfit (at the hem).

Hose should be worn with all but the most casual clothing. Bare legs are never appropriate with tailored or dressy things.

Gloves should be worn with a hat, except when eating, drinking, or in a church service. Remove gloves just prior to and put back on immediately after these named exceptions.

Taffeta, velvet, satin, *peau de soie*, etc., are generally considered *evening only* fabrics, as are those with metallic threads. Any of these, of course, may appropriately appear as trim on daytime wear. Tailored velvet jackets are considered "in" at the moment for day wear;

they are still on the dressy end of the scale, and best worn when going non-stop from day to evening activities.

Hats are basically considered daytime wear, with 5 p.m. being their curfew, except for the small, dressy evening hat variously in and out of fashion. (If, however, it is the custom of your church to wear hats whenever in a service, do so!)

The "tone" of an outfit should be consistent throughout—that is, casual and dressy items should not be mixed.

For those special occasions when you're given a corsage, be sure you wear it the correct way: with the flowers in the position in which they naturally grow. In other words, the ribbon portion of the corsage will be below the flowers.

There are three basic terms with which to be familiar in order to dress appropriately: tailored, casual, and dressy.

Tailored clothing has a crisp, businesslike appearance. It is characterized by generally straight, simple lines and conservative, "background" feel in fabrics and in colors—such as gray, brown, camel, and navy.

Blouses—pointed or rounded collars; jabot-tied self-scarf; slim-cut, shirt look.

Jackets—medium length; lines skimming, not hugging the body; shoulder seams fall at shoulder line, not "dropped." No excess trims. Buttons and belting of self color and/or fabric. Blazers.

Skirts—straight or A-line (gathering at waist

adds softness and dressiness to appearance).

Dresses—conservative "background" colors; generally self-trimmed. Straight or A-line skirts. Simple, clean-lined bodice design.

Shoes—medium heel height; unadorned plain pump in basic or "background" colors.

Bags—medium size; basic or "background" colors; neat appearance.

Casual apparel gives a "country living" feel to your appearance. Silhouette allows for freedom of movement.

Fabrics—synthetic blends; cottons; novelty weaves and textures; wools in bulky, nubby, and "cuddly" textures.

Colors and patterns—bold, bright, light.

Blouses—drop-shoulder; sleeveless; bowed ties. (Sweaters are almost always casual.)

Skirts—gathered, gored, full, or wrap.

Dresses—necks of varying shapes (round, square, peter pan); sleeveless, three-quarter, or long.

Trim—contrast and highlight by fabrics and color.

Shoes—colored; leather sandals; canvas; cork heels; stacked heels; fat heels; wedge heels.

Bags—large; accent colors; straw; novelty.

Dressy attire conveys the special-occasion feel. Various levels of formality within the general category, covering a "church dressy" to "banquet dressy."

Fabrics—silk, crepe; drapable; shiny.

Colors—deeps, darks. (It's sometimes helpful to borrow from the masculine rule of thumb: the more formal the occasion, the darker the outfit should be.)

Silhouette—drapings, flounces, shawl collars.

Blouses—shiny fabrics; metallic threads; lace trims; ruffles.

Skirts—range from very full to very slim; draped.

Dresses—bateau or cowl prominent among necklines.

Shoes—patent and very shiny leathers; silk, faille, gold or silver (latter two are *evening only*); slender, high heels; slender-strapped heeled sandals; fancy buckle or bow trim.

Bags—small; clutch or evening type; patent leather; beaded or with jeweled ornamentation.

The frustrating thing about such a listing is that it's impossible to cover everything. Within each general category, too, there are different degrees of application. Also, the characteristics of one category may sometimes be transposed to another; but I've tried to make a listing of item/characteristics *most frequently* true to their own category.

The woman who represents the Lord Jesus Christ has a responsibility to look her appropriate best at all times. Wise, careful building and use of a wardrobe can greatly aid toward that worthy goal.

APPEARANCE ABUSES

Closets and their contents can be misused and abused by Christian women as well as by unsaved. Many times the former do so on the matter of age and what constitutes appropriateness thereto.

A woman who claims to know Christ as her Saviour comes across as being singularly unattractive if she is unable to accept and enjoy whatever age she happens to be. Both men and women are guilty of "age sham," but women seem particularly prone toward it.

A girl who paints maturity onto her face or feigns it by a premature sophistication of clothing is a pitiable individual. She robs herself of her fleeting, beautiful youth and rushes toward an embittered maturity—for she'll realize her mistake only when it's too late.

Conversely, a matron who bundles herself into bows and frills and little-girl curls, actions, and voice, only pulls off a pathetic charade in daylight and faces starker reality at her midnight mirror. So, too, the grandmother who dresses and dyes, paints and poses like a siren.

Whatever our age, if we yearn and sigh for some age bracket other than our own, we're abusing the gift of time the Lord has so graciously given us. We are stewards of time just as we are stewards of our talents. To try to wrench and twist it out of shape is to fail in our stewardship, thereby disappointing our Lord.

But let's get into some specifics. There are several distinct areas in which a girl or woman tries to appear an age other then her own. The first of these is cosmetics. Youth is the time when the color in a woman's face is naturally high. The last thing in the world she needs is gobs of make-up. In trying to look "mature" *a la* the paint pot, a girl only succeeds in spoiling youth's beauty and making herself look hard. On the other hand, an older woman who "paints" beyond subtle enhancement to the desperate reach for youth only draws attention to the artifice and the real age she's trying so hard to hide.

The second area in which women deny their true age is in clothing. The young girl hankers for "sophisticated" clothes instead of the school-girl variety, whereas the age-denying grand-mother squeezes herself into a wasp-waisted, frilly number that only accentuates her age-softened physique.

Nor does hair escape the pretenders' arts. The young girl labors long and hard with curling irons and combs to force her free-swinging young hair into a "mature" style seen on TV. What a waste! The grandmother is simulta-neously spending hours and dollars in the beauty parlor for extreme dye jobs which don't fool anyone and usually make her look older; *or* she lets the natural gray show but lets her hair fall to her shoulders in a hark-back to high school days: either attempt at youth-capturing is highly unbecoming and only succeeds in raising eye-brows or pity.

Finally, conduct may be affected by a woman's reluctance to accept her age. The girl assumes the walk, mannerisms, and voice of some older woman she thinks "glamorous"— while the matron puts on a nonstop performance of the cute, simpering, sweet little thing she was forty years ago.

We live in a strange day when "glamour" is tantalizingly presented by the media in such a way that both young and older women strive to attain it at the expense of enjoying and enhancing their own age. Girls are particularly susceptible to the patent, slick "woman-of-the-world" look. Unfortunately, concomitant with the "look" comes world-hardened attitudes and actions. The older woman falls for the unceasing touting of youth. We are told, directly or by inference, that "young" is great, and "old" is gruesome.

Christian girls should enjoy being girls, appreciating the freshness and simplicity of life, while at the same time recognizing God's claims upon their youth: "Be thou an *example* of the believer." The older woman should be so filled with thanksgiving at the Lord's goodness in the time He has allowed her that she treasures the years and reflects the mellowing they have done in her spirit, mind, and emotions. For her, Scripture says plainly that she should "Teach the younger women." And how desperately those younger ones need the instruction of her *living example*!

Wherever we Christian women are along the road of life, we need to stop and take honest stock of our reactions to the milestones that mark the way. Are we resenting them, and thereby displeasing the Lord? Are we denying the fruitfulness of the now we could so greatly

enjoy by yearning for the unattainable past or
future? We need to say, with the Psalmist,

> So teach us to number our days, that we
> may apply our hearts unto wisdom.
> (Psalm 90:12)

Spiritual wisdom will make us see ourselves and
our ages aright, and it will enable us to use our
hours and days as we ought.

Personal Pinpointing

1. My closet now   (contains/does not contain)
clothing which is immodest.
Below is a listing which will designate what
garment(s), what the specific problem is with
that piece of clothing to make it immodest, and
what can be done to remedy the problem:

Garment(s)	Problem(s)	Remedy
_____	_____	_____
_____	_____	_____
_____	_____	_____
_____	_____	_____
_____	_____	_____
_____	_____	_____
_____	_____	_____

2. In analyzing the following,
    a. Region: _____
    b. Locale: _____
    c. Focus of endeavor: _____

    d. Social activities: _____

I come to the conclusion that my wardrobe emphasis should be:

	Mostly	*Some*	*Very Few*
casual	_____	_____	_____
tailored	_____	_____	_____
dressy	_____	_____	_____
washables	_____	_____	_____
dry-cleanables	_____	_____	_____
subdued colors	_____	_____	_____
dark colors	_____	_____	_____
light colors	_____	_____	_____
bright colors	_____	_____	_____

3. My figure can be enhanced by color/tone minimization in the _____ area.

4. Clothing lines which are not good for my figure are: _____
_____
_____

5. My basic winter color: _____

6. My basic summer color: _____

Spiritual Balance

In the opening of this chapter, I mentioned the matter of *proportion* in our womanly interest in clothing. We will keep our priorities straight if we consistently put our eyes and emphasis upon the clothing of our souls. Meditate much upon that blessed passage in Isaiah which reads,

> I will greatly rejoice in the Lord, my soul shall be joyful in my God; for he hath clothed me with the garments of salvation, he hath covered me with the robe of righteousness, as a bridegroom decketh himself with ornaments, and as a bride adorneth herself with her jewels.
>
> (Isaiah 61:10)

7

That Awesome Audio

"Ooooops—what's *this* subject doing in here?" you may ask. The answer is that your speech is an integral part of the "picture" you present to the world. I've known more than a few women whose really lovely exteriors were nullified when they opened their mouths. The mouth provides clues to a woman's real self, and it influences others' reactions.

How about *you*? Does your voice, like fingernails scraping a chalkboard, cause people to shiver? Or do you frequently hear, "Pardon me, what was that you said?" Do your children comment that you always sound angry? If those or other negative reactions meet you in the everyday round of life, this chapter can prove especially beneficial to you. But *all* of us need to take time to think about our speech—its sound and its contents.

SOUND

Most of us take our voices for granted. But our entire speech mechanism is a marvelous part of God's human creation. Voices have several distinct characteristics; in order to make them really meaningful to you, you need to hear your own voice from the outside, as others do. Ask someone to make a recording of your speech when you're not aware of it. Then *really listen* to yourself. Also enlist the aid of two or three friends who love you enough and care sufficiently about the impression you make on other people to tell you the truth.

Now, keeping your voice recording handy, consider the quality of the sound you produce, its overall "feel." An unlovely quality grates on ears and nerves alike. Desirable characteristics are richness and pleasantness. William Shakespeare well described a lovely feminine voice in King Lear's line, "Her voice was ever soft, gentle, and low—an excellent thing in woman." More importantly, remember that Scripture directs Christian women to have a "meek and quiet spirit"; harsh vocal quality belies such a spirit. Most of us need to strive to incorporate gentleness into our voices. But in trying to overcome vocal unpleasantness, don't swing to a breathy, little-girl quality. Breathy Beulah comes across as being a phony or slightly unbright, neither of which serves as an attractive advertisement for Christianity!

Second, consider projection. How loudly— or softly—do you habitually speak? A loudmouthed woman is a walking abomination. No matter how good her heart, she deafens and disgusts her poor hearers by her megaphone tones. Loudness translates as brazenness—a far cry from the gentleness a bornagain woman should convey! If you habitually speak too loudly, by all means re-learn your vocal habits. Give the ears of your loved ones and acquaintances a well-deserved break. On the other hand, your projection shouldn't be so anemic that you sound sick and your "hearers" can't hear you!

Pitch is a third consideration. It has to do with the basic placement of your voice on a musical scale. There are, of course, great variations in habitual pitches from person to person. The extremes for a woman to avoid are the super-low voice whose huskiness comes across as a "whiskey voice," and the super-high voice that sounds like a mouse with its tail stepped on. Don't try to alter your basic pitch drastically, forcing yourself into an unnatural and uncomfortable register. But if you have an unpleasant pitch, a slight adjustment in habitual level can add greatly to your "listenability."

Pace is the fourth area where we can work to improve our audible image. We should neither rattle at machine-gun rate nor drag so slowly through our sentences that listeners snore between words and phrases. The racing rate makes us sound brainless; the dragging rate communicates our being too lazy to live. Either end of the pace spectrum will cause listeners to turn us off—it's just not worth the effort!

Enunciation, or word formation, is the fifth and final aspect of vocal characteristics that need a check-up. We produce a wide range of speech sounds by minute adjustments in jaw, lips, tongue, soft palate, and teeth. Most of us know how to form our sounds correctly; but we grow lazy and careless. For example, we often reduce -ng endings on words to -n'—as in runnin', comin', etc. Or we produce our consonants so carelessly that people find it hard to understand our words: e.g., "stan'art" for "standard." Perhaps, though, rather than laziness or carelessness, your particular problem is a regional dialect so thick it makes your speech unintelligible to hearers who speak General American. Whatever our shortcomings in enunciation, we need to spend some time and effort polishing them in acceptable, understandable form.

You *can* improve your vocal characteristics. Take the matter to the Lord, ask family and friends to remind you when your particular vocal fault creeps in, and practice, practice, practice the *best* voice you can produce. Use your travel time or housework hours; talk to the vacuum while you clean or to the bathtub while you scour. To multiply the effectiveness of your practice, use Scripture verses as your practice material: you will benefit not only your speech, but also your spirit. Your goal is not a sweety-sweet, o-ver-ly-pre-cise speech: the first effect is saccharine, the second snooty. Instead, you merely need to replace poor vocal habits with good ones. Speech is a learned skill—and learning can be embellished and corrected. A pleasant, well-modulated, easily-heard and -understood voice projects a positive image of your personality, your character, and your Lord.

CONTENT

A Christian woman should be a *lady*—not just in her bearing and appearance, but in her speech as well. Good grammar is a must for a lady. Poor grammar reflects not so much a woman's level of education as her level of concern. Proper grammar doesn't really come from a classroom; it springs from caring how you handle your native language. Poor grammar and slovenly character are automatically connected in the mind of a knowledgeable hearer. In an era when the unsaved consciously or unconsciously express their rebellion against discipline and traditionalism by flaunting the rules of grammar, Christians should be doubly careful to *adhere* to those rules! The breakdown of our language is symptomatic of the breakdown of our society: a believer should be the last person in the world guilty of condoning or contributing to that declension. Some people mistakenly feel that bad grammar projects a "folksy" image. But, to put it bluntly in their own jargon, "Them just ain't the folks that really gets to most folks!" Good grammatical construction, like good manners, is acceptable at every social level; poor grammar severely limits your social mobility— and that in turn limits your effectiveness as a witness for Christ. Maybe some of you married women say, "I hardly even get out of the house! About the only people I talk to are my kids!" What do you mean, "only"? What greater reason could there be for using good grammar? Your children may learn the *rules* of grammar at school—but they'll learn their *use* of grammar at home. What are you teaching them?

If you have a problem with grammar, *do* something about it! Towns large and small offer night and/or mini-courses for adults in English. Or go back to your old schoolbooks for concentrated review and practice. If you are still in school, *concentrate* in those English classes. Whatever it takes, do whip your grammar into good shape and keep it that way.

Moving on to further consideration of your speech content, I challenge you to record faithfully, for a full week, (a) how much you talk and (b) what you talk about. Then at the end of the week, sit down and think seriously about your findings.

One of the most unlovely traits a born-again woman can have speechwise is that of being a blabbermouth. If your jaw has the tendency to run non-stop and in high gear, you need to put the brakes on it—*hard*. Chances are you've either driven the people around you to distraction, or they've switched to another channel. Chances are also good that in your gabbing you've talked of things you had no business discussing: spreading "Have you heards" and "Did you knows" left and right like feathers from a torn pillow. If a flapping tongue is characteristic of you, make an in-depth study of it as Scripture handles the subject. Dwell, for instance, on the interesting company in which God places the loose-tongued person:

> But let none of you suffer as a murderer, or as a thief, or as a busybody in other men's matters. (I Peter 4:15)

It's virtually impossible to come out of such a Bible study without the Holy Spirit's conviction at work on your heart—and then you will go to work on your jaw.

Look again at your content/quantity chart. What is the predominant *mood* of your speech? Gloom and doom? Griping? Criticism? Argumentativeness? All those are unattractive and undesirable in a Christian *because they indicate heart mood*. (Matthew 12:34b, "For out of the abundance of the heart the mouth speaketh.") That powerful truth should drive us to our knees and to our Bibles. The Word will quickly show what our Heavenly Father thinks about our spiritual/speech shadings. For example, how can we cast gloom abroad with our lips when we're told to "Rejoice evermore" (I Thessalonians 5:16)? And "Do all things without murmurings and disputings" (Philippians 2:14) immediately wipes out both griping and argumentativeness. In condemning criticism, Scripture accurately applies the descriptive word, "backbiting." Having had such heavy artillery pounding away at the negative moods of our speech, we need to ask the Lord to fill the gaps with their spiritual opposites:

    —optimism to replace gloom

    —rejoicing to replace griping

    —longsuffering and a charitable spirit to replace criticism

    —submission to replace argumentativeness.

Take still another look at your speech-study chart. What are the *subjects* of your conversations? Soap opera developments? Lurid unsavory stories from magazines and newspapers? If so, you are violating the Scriptural injunction to think on beautiful, wholesome things. (Remember Philippians 4:8?) A garbage-fed heart is bound to result in a garbage-spewing mouth: a deplorable attribute which denies the Christian woman the right to be called a lady!

As with the characteristics of your speech, so too with its contents: you need not—and should not—remain as you are. Instead, repenting of the junk food you've been shoveling into your heart, you should get rid of it and replace it with the milk and meat of God's Word, meditating on things of the Lord, reading of Christian and *good* literature, and listening to good music.

Having thought about your speech as an individual consideration, let's now concentrate upon its social aspects, as well. How do you interact vocally with others: how are your *conversational* skills? It takes more than just an open mouth to make a good conversationalist. Your talking with others is important—because you cause some kind of reaction from them and because you reveal volumes about yourself.

There are four "sweeteners" all of us need to insert frequently into our speech (FIRST of all in our homes!): "Please," "Thank you," "Pardon me," and "I'm sorry." What a world of difference they can make in our daily contact! Don't *you* react more pleasurably and compliantly to someone who is polite rather than brusque?

Conversation is *not* a monologue. Don't be guilty of hogging the conversational ball; it's supposed to bounce back and forth freely among all members of a group. Stop right here and ask yourself a hard question, then answer it— honestly: "Am I a bore?" None of us wants to be boring to others, but many, nonetheless, win high rewards for boresmanship. Here are some specific conversational traits characteristic of bores.

Talking too much. Some people are so enamored of their own yacking that they never let anyone else get a word in edgewise.

Bragging. What an unbecoming speech habit for a Christian! Single women boast of their sexual, professional, or scholastic exploits while married women brag about their children: the sweetest, smartest, best-mannered, most original, most spiritual, beautiful, successful, blah, blah, blah. . . .Ugh!

Including unnecessary details. It takes some people ten minutes to tell you how they crossed Main Street yesterday—because in the process they have to explain the manner of their birth, the weather conditions, the various circumstances that brought them to Main Street, the life history of Great Uncle Henry who lives on that street, etc.

Talking only with the confines of your own small world. A mention of husband and children is fine—but don't dump truckloads of information about them every time we meet! All of us need to expand our mental horizons through reading, travel, etc., so that our "conversational comfort zone" expands accordingly.

Dwelling on the past. Some people respond to a simple "How are you today?" with a blow-by-blow harking back to their beginnings!

For some girls and women reading this book, the problem is *hiding from* the conversational ball, not hogging it. But consider for a moment: neither one makes for much of a ball game! "But I'm so timid," you sigh. Timidity afflicts many of us, and it most often springs from poor self-image. Naturally, she who low-rates herself is convinced that others share her evaluation. Her approach to social situations, therefore, is very hesitant and fearful. She ducks mentally whenever the conversational ball heads her way, terrified lest she utter a comment or question to reveal her imagined faults and foibles. For every Timid Timothea reading this chapter, a few special words: Go again to those Bible passages pointed out in Chapter Three indicating your uniqueness and specialness in God's eyes. Ask the Lord to give you a firm mental and emotional grip on the picture *He* paints of you in those verses. Then ask Him to help you realize that mere human beings (foremost among whom is *you!*) have twisted your internal self-portrait, making you feel stupid, ugly, lacking in abilities, or whatever. Now: which picture should you accept?

Having rearranged your mental picture gallery, re-work your concept of social situations: they are not dreadful, nerve-straining occasions holding ghastly threats for you. They are rich opportunities to meet new friends, to enjoy the interchange of ideas, to bask in the warmth of human companionship and Christian fellowship. And determine that *you will be friendly*. (Proverbs 18:24 reminds us, "A man that hath friends must shew himself friendly.") People may have judged you to be "cold" or "aloof" because of the restraint put upon you by timidity. There is no way for them to adjust that misconception unless you're willing to come out from behind the walls of protective silence and allow the real, warm, valuable and interesting YOU to be revealed.

Whether talking with an individual or a group, *eye contact* is very important. Don't look at the other person's hair, her left ear, her mouth, or over her shoulder—look her in the eye! Avoiding eye contact gives the impression of having something to hide and is an indication of weak character. When you're talking to a group of people, take each of them into your eye contact; doing so includes them all in the focus of your attention, giving no one a "left out" feeling.

A believer's conversation should always observe standards of propriety. Open discussion of any and all subjects is the order of the day among the unsaved—but for Christian women there are things that should not be discussed in mixed groups, and there are some matters that are inappropriate for open discussion—any time, any place—*period*! This is part of what the Bible calls being "discreet" (Titus 2:5).

Don't be a name-dropper. The person who drops such lines as, "When I was with Senator Smith last week. . ." or "Yesterday when I was eating with Dr. Important. . ." is a little person trying to enlarge her own image. It fools no one; it's simply tiresome.

Do, by all means develop the ability to *listen*! Be genuinely interested in other people and in what they have to say. Learning to listen puts the emphasis where it ought to be in conversation—on others rather than on yourself.

It is not only in face-to-face conversation that we need to take care; telephone manners are likewise of great importance. On the telephone, all the caller has as an impression of you is your voice—no facial expression, no body language, nothing to help him interpret your meaning, attitude, situation, and character. That means your tone and inflections are everything! Remember—the caller doesn't know you're standing there with the kids pulling the house down around your ears; or that you've had one of the worst days of your entire life; or that you've just had a knock-down-drag-out fight with your husband. Being totally ignorant, he will feel stung by your icy or irate tones.

As a final consideration in the matter of conversation, all our social contacts should be marked by *tactfulness*. Tact has been defined as "the delicate perception of the right thing to say or do *without offending*." An offense is a hurt. Therefore tactlessness is actually cruelty; how can that be rightly characteristic of Christianity? The only offense we are ever to give is that of the *cross*—not of our own crassness! We've all experienced the piercing wound made by an inconsiderate remark or question. Tactfulness avoids giving such a wound. Following are a few examples of instances wherein tact needs to be employed.

Don't say "I know your face, but I just can't remember your name." That says, in essence, "Sorry, Dearie, but you really weren't worth remembering." Instead, make it clear that *you* are to blame, saying simply, "I'm very sorry, but I've forgotten your name."

Don't ask questions which infringe upon a person's privacy. Women are especially liable to offend in this because of feminine curiosity. If a person volunteers information concerning something which is a part of her private life, that's her business. But never probe.

Don't talk about subjects which might bring pain to another. A workable maxim is , "Never talk of ropes to a man whose father has been hanged."

Don't compliment one person in a group to the exclusion of others. To comment to one in a group of fifteen women, "Oh, I just love that dress; you look perfectly beautiful!" makes all the others feel like Daisy Dowdies.

Don't talk about a social function which only a part of the group attended (or plans to attend). That's painful to those not invited.

Don't ask questions or make comments which injure a person's feelings about himself. In other words, don't be the type who makes "cute" remarks such as, "Well, well—didn't get enough oatmeal as a child, did you, Shrimp?" Or, "Yipes! With the size of those ears, you'd better avoid strong winds, or you'll fly." *You* may get a laugh out of such unkind comments—but the object of them will feel miserable. Very frequently, the characteristic or attribute chosen as the butt of the "smart" remark is the very thing the person already feels self-conscious about; your reminder will add greatly to his pain.

Don't answer a direct question in such a way as to wound the questioner. For instance, a dear little old lady comes up to you at a church supper and asks, "How did you like my pie?" It was awful; but to be bluntly—and cruelly—truthful would deeply injure the dear lady's heart. But as a Christian you must *not* lie. The situation can be salvaged by non-specific words like "interesting," "different," or "unique"— then move on to a sincere compliment for something about the person or thing, such as,

"... and what I always enjoy so much about your pies is how *pretty* they are!"

One final reminder—*you* are not the important person in Christian conversation: the *other person* is. Your concentration on and consideration of the other person will not only be welcomed, but it will also thaw your timidity-stalled brain so you can help put him at ease.

It is appropriate to remind you that the Christian woman's avoiding offense in conversation is *not* to be carried into the realm of cowardice. In other words, while we realize we should not offend personally, we must simultaneously remember to faithfully bear testimony—and *the gospel will bring offense*. There must never be spiritual compromise in conversation: that denies the Lord Who bought us! The scriptural injunction is, "Let your speech be always with grace, seasoned with salt, that ye may know how ye ought to answer every man" (Colossians 4:6). The "grace" is compassionate consideration; the "salt" loyalty to and proclamation of God's Word.

The woman who exercises her Christian principles in conversation will not only be remembered as a charming person; she will also be enriched herself as she reaches out through the tool of conversation to gain knowledge and understanding of others.

Personal Pinpointing

1. I would most accurately describe my voice as:

a. Quality: _____
(rich/average/thin/pleasant/harsh/breathy/
hoarse/gutteral)

b. Projection: _____
(loud/adequate/weak)

c. Pitch: _____
(very high/high/mid-range/low/very low)

d. Pace: _____
(rushed/staccato/average/slow/very slow)

e. Enunciation:

Substitutions: _____

Dropped sounds: _____

Distorted sounds: _____

2. The main content problem I have with my speech is _____ .

3. My best quality as a conversationalist is __
_____

4. My poorest characteristic as a conversationalist is _____
_____

Spiritual Balance

Our human conversations will take on the proper characteristics as we are faithful in maintaining the lines of communication with our Lord. As we spend time daily in private devotions, talking to Him and letting Him talk to us through His Word, His Holy Spirit's presence in our hearts will become increasingly evident—and the love for others which is His characteristic will become ours, as well. It is right there—in the heart and spirit—that the source of Christian conversational attributes lies.

8

The Manners Message

We have a friend whose highest commendation lies in the phrase, "She has beautiful manners." That statement has always intrigued me, and over the years I've come to appreciate the wisdom of choosing that measurement as indicative of attractiveness rather than face or personality. Either face or personality is a gift of the Lord for which no woman can claim credit—but good manners come from *concern for other people* and *disciplined learning and practice*: characteristics of a beautiful spirit.

A good definition of etiquette is "correct conduct under all circumstances of life." That takes manners off the "just-for-company" shelf and puts them into day-in-day-out action!

Everyone *has* manners—but they range from abominable to admirable. What makes the difference in the quality of mannerly conduct?

Social standing? Talent? Training? The answer to each of those is no: the difference lies within the person—in the spirit which motivates his social conduct. The key to etiquette is *consideration for others*.

Dr. Bob Jones Sr. said, "You do what you do because you are what you are." Since good manners are a demonstration of thoughtfulness, poor manners indicate an unfeeling or even scornful attitude. For a believer claiming to live in accordance with scriptural principles, insensitivity and scornfulness are supposed to be off-limits! Loving others as you love yourself will move you to do all you can to put them at their ease; to demonstrate kindness through your actions. The result will be proper social conduct—in other words, etiquette!

In undertaking a manners-polishing program, you can encourage yourself by a reminder that *everyone* must learn manners; they are not inborn. Self-centeredness is a human trait evident from early babyhood: we have to *learn* to think of others. Learning etiquette will require two things of you: personal effort and outward-directed concern.

But, you may argue, why should I adopt an etiquette-improvement program? Think for a moment: we are all social creatures; we don't live as hermits—and social life at every level puts demands upon us that expose our life-guiding principles. There are three outstanding reasons for making etiquette a part of you:

First, etiquette is important **for your own**

self-confidence and ease. Few circumstances are more uncomfortable than being in a social situation where you're unsure of proper conduct. A good grasp of etiquette, therefore, can eliminate considerable wear and tear on your worry system.

Second, etiquette is vitally important **to the comfort and enjoyment of others**. If your manners are uncouth, the people around you are going to be offended; even revolted. If your manners are passable but you're tense from trying to maintain rigid "company behavior," the company is going to sense that tension and in turn be made uneasy.

Third and most important of all, etiquette is important **to your testimony**. Proper social conduct is a demonstration of the scriptural principles of (a) loving others, (b) living an example, and (c) letting Christ be seen through you. Your manners count *for* or *against* your Saviour. If an unsaved person is nauseated by your table manners, don't think for a minute he's going to be interested in the faith you claim to represent!

A good verse to memorize in connection with etiquette is I Peter 2:9, "But ye are a chosen generation, a royal priesthood, an holy nation, a peculiar people; that ye should shew forth the praises of him who hath called you out of darkness into his marvellous light." Notice that phrase, "shew forth"—not just "talk forth"! That means your *conduct* is to be a testimony. We who know Christ as Saviour are children of the

King of Heaven—as such, we haven't any excuse
for slovenly conduct.

A final few reminders before getting into
some etiquette specifics. Good manners depend
not so much on the rules as on the reasons
behind the rules. Common sense, too, plays an
important role in social behavior. That's a handy
thought to fall back on when you don't know
specifically what to do in a situation: what action
would *common sense* plus *consideration* prescribe? It
is also very important to remember that *the lady
always sets the standard*! Do you resent the sloppy
manners of your boyfriend or husband? Check
up on your own conduct. Someone has well said
that a lady is a woman who lets a man enjoy
being a gentleman.

TABLE ETIQUETTE

We get a proper idea of the importance of
table manners by realizing that large corpora-
tions considering hiring or promoting someone
for a responsible position will take that person
and his wife out for a meal—and watch their
table manners. What is seen at the table can
either work for or against their winning the
position—because the company knows the
person in that position represents the company.
How much weightier is our representation of
our Saviour and Lord!

In the following discussion, only a very few
items can be covered. I would urge you to brush
up on the subject of etiquette by reading a
complete book on the subject. In this chapter, I

can touch only on items which loom largest in necessity and practicality for people with "average" school activities.

Seating

As a lady, you should always wait for the gentleman's assistance. If he is not immediately attentive to the task, simply stand quietly waiting. There are always occasions when the men at the table have more than one woman to assist; that's going to take a few seconds. Don't feel awkward standing there waiting your turn; it should be an easy, natural situation in which you do *not* glare or dart glances of "Hurry up, for pity's sake!" There is a common-sense exception: if the men are strongly outnumbered at the table and your place is several women away from one of the overworked gentlemen, go ahead and seat yourself.

When the gentleman approaches to help you, step to the side of the chair opposite the direction of his approach. That is, if he comes from your left, step to the right of your chair. You have thus cleared the way for him to pull the chair away from the table. Then, slip into the chair from the side to which you've moved.

Remember that the gentleman is going to move the chair (and you) toward the table. So don't descend onto the chair like the Rock of Gibralter. Take your seat, then use your thigh muscles to partially lift your weight as he scoots the chair forward. If the poor man has to bodily heave you and chair closer to the table, he's courting back strain!

Serving and passing

Food moves *toward the right* around the table. (The only exception is when someone asks for a particular dish and it is much closer to pass it to the left rather than to the right.) There is a proper way to receive and pass food in its trip around the table:

(a) receive dish or platter with your *right* hand (crossing your body with that arm),

(b) transfer serving piece to your *left* hand for holding while you serve yourself, and

(c) pass the food to the person on your right with your *left* hand (again, crossing your body with your arm in the process). This method of receiving and passing has been universally adopted because it is the most considerate of those sitting to either side of you, since it reduces the possibility of your hitting them with an elbow or arm. Also, by giving you greater strength and control than a "backhand" pass, it helps you to avoid spills.

In serving yourself, take only enough food for a moderate-sized helping. Consider the hunger pangs of the rest of the people at the table!

Always use the serving utensil provided— never your own fork or spoon—to take the food from the serving vessel. Nobody wants your germs or food bits!

Never take food from platter or bowl without taking the serving vessel. Haven't you responded, say, to a request for the rolls—then had the asker take a roll and leave you holding the platter? Pretty clear expression of thought-lessness and ingratitude, isn't it?

Don't stop the food's progress around the table. Some people serve themselves, then put the platter or bowl on the table, never considering those farther along who've not yet been served.

If you are a guest at a meal where the host or hostess serves the plates, it is proper to indicate your desire for a smaller-than-average portion of a particular food.

Use of silverware

How do you react when sitting down to a table at which various sizes and shapes of silver pieces appear on both sides of the plates? With dread as you realize you don't know what utensil to use for which food? With panic and self-consciousness? Those negative reactions can be laid to rest by the knowledge of two simple principles: (a) use silver working *from the outside in* toward the plate, and (b) watch the hostess for cues. Since a picture is worth a thousand words, study this diagram to see the outside-in principle:

water

salad
dinner
dessert

soup

Inevitably, there will be times when you're unsure how a particular food is to be eaten. In such instances, unobtrusively watch your hostess.

Many people don't know how to wield the silver once they decide which piece is proper. The most-often-broken rule of correct usage comes with an ordinary knife and fork.

Incorrect silver usage gives offense—no matter how artfully a little finger may be cocked! Perhaps the very harshness of that statement is needed to awaken you to your responsibility: consider—and re-learn, if need be—the proper handling of a knife and fork:

A fork should be neither a dagger (a) nor a shovel (b):

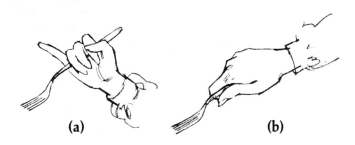

(a)   (b)

The proper way to hold a fork or spoon:

Use the *only* correct method for cutting:

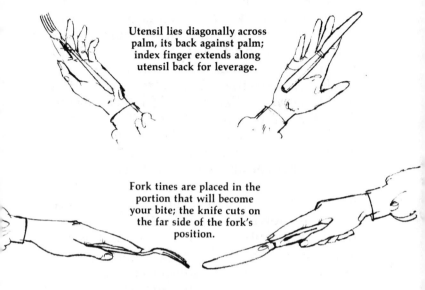

Utensil lies diagonally across palm, its back against palm; index finger extends along utensil back for leverage.

Fork tines are placed in the portion that will become your bite; the knife cuts on the far side of the fork's position.

Note: Those who are left-handed will simply reverse hands, but use the identical positions/techniques.

If you have never had the opportunity to learn the proper handling of a knife and fork, *learn it now and make it habitual*. Few changes of behavior have such power to add cultural polish to your social image.

Cut only one piece of meat at a time. To cut more than one bite conveys the idea of ravening hunger.

When not using your knife for cutting, it should rest "cornered" across the plate rim. The handle should *not* rest on the table.

Eating

Keep your left hand (right hand, if you're left-handed) in your lap while eating, except when you have to cut, butter bread, steady a dish, etc. You do *not* need to prop yourself up on your non-active arm while eating.

Remember that silverware is for eating—not for *gesturing*. Particles of food can easily be slung from a waving fork or knife.

It is permissible to cut unwieldly chunks of lettuce, tomato, etc., in your salad.

If you encounter something in a meal which is not cuttable, what should you do? Make a clever comment about "shoe-leather meat"? Choke it down uncut? Neither. Keep your cutting attempts inconspicuous, and without calling attention to your difficulties, simply leave the stubborn portion on your plate.

Avoid stuffing your mouth—either by taking overlarge bites or by "piggybacking"—adding a bite before having chewed and swallowed a prior bite completely. A stuffed mouth is grossly unattractive. But, don't go to the other extreme of "itty bitty" bites whereby it takes more than one bite to empty a fork. That is not a sign of delicacy or femininity—only of silliness. The rule is to take a moderate amount of food onto your fork or spoon, and to empty that utensil in one bite or sip.

Your dinner napkin should lie half-opened on your lap (or fully opened if it's a dessert-sized napkin).

Always chew *with your lips closed*. No one

wants to see or hear you prepare your food for your stomach!

In eating soup, tip and move the soup spoon *away* from you. That's to prevent the shovel-it-in look. It is permissible to tip the cup or bowl to get the last drops of a liquid food—but the vessel should be tipped away from you.

Never talk with your mouth full. It can result in spraying your table companion with partially-masticated food or bring on choking. Keeping this rule in mind, avoid asking someone a question while his mouth is full. If someone should ask you a question while you're chewing, silently indicate (napkin-to-lips gesture, for example) that you need a moment before you can reply.

Cut and manage your food neatly. By all means, don't pre-mix it on your plate. Sure, everyone knows it will eventually get mixed; but let the blending take place in the out-of-sight location the Lord intended!

What about getting something in your mouth that's unchewable? You certainly shouldn't attempt to swallow the hunk whole. "Cafe coronary" (choking to death) can result from that unwise decision. Instead, unobtrusively remove the offending portion from your mouth and return it to the plate. Do not call attention to your plight—you will thereby embarrass your hostess, who has spent a good deal of time, effort, and money preparing the meal.

Always maintain good posture while eating.

Don't be guilty of the "supper slump" or the "lunchtime lurch". Sit tall while you eat, so your appearance is one of refinement.

There are several foods that are a special challenge to eat. Perhaps foremost among them is spaghetti. Delicious as it is, nearly every bite results in dangling, awkward, spattering strands. Of course you *can* hoist the white flag of surrender by cutting spaghetti into fork-size length. But that's considered cowardly. There is, however, a method for eating spaghetti which gives as neat consumption as possible. It is a two-handed approach: The fork in held in your right hand (for left-handedness, just reverse the whole description); your left hand holds a large-bowled spoon. Take a few strands of spaghetti on your fork, then place the ends of the fork tines in the spoon and turn the fork over and over so the spaghetti is rolled around the fork tines. When most of the strands have been thus captured, take the bite to your mouth. Almost inevitably there will be one or two danglers, but they will be far fewer than in other methods.

Authorities on etiquette consider fried chicken to be finger food. An exception to that general statement, however, would be an oversized piece (which should be eaten with a fork) or a situation where the hostess is using knife and fork. (You as a guest are obliged to do so, too.)

Then there are olives with pits intact. How to eat them gracefully? Take the whole olive into your mouth and eat the meat from the seed.

Then move the seed to the very front of your mouth (lips closed, tongue doing the moving work); then, using thumb and forefinger, remove the pit and place it to one side on your plate.

Finishing a meal

When you have completed your meal, place knife, fork and spoon across the middle or upper half of your plate, with handles parallel to the table's edge. A seafood fork would also be placed across the dinner plate, unless the fish course had been removed earlier. A soup spoon may be left in the soup bowl or on its service plate.

There is no need to re-fold your napkin as neatly as it appeared at the meal's start. Your hostess knows it has been used! Leave the napkin beside your plate in a crumpled or lightly folded form.

Elbows should never be on the table while you're eating; but once the meal is finished, elbows may rest on the table in order to facilitate conversation.

SOCIAL ETIQUETTE

Social grace. The goal you should pursue in giving attention to social skills is the development of social grace: *the ability to appear comfortably at ease in any situation.* A vital component of social grace is poise. Fortunately, poise is not so much a matter of how you feel as how you appear. Those characterized by poise have learned a tri-partite formula: quietness + control + concentration on others. Let's consider just how these three elements combine to create poise.

Quietness. Both physically and vocally you need to apply that part of the formula. Fidgeting, nervous mannerisms, loud or abundant talking all telegraph an unmistakable message: nervousness. Replacing those traitorous telegraphers with quietness totally changes the message you send. Instead of considering you nervous or ill at ease, those around you will judge you to be poised.

Control. No one can appear poised who is not in control. Somehow, the pressure of social occasions seems to loosen a person's control, and negative personality traits blossom forth: the timid person withdraws more than ever, whereas the extrovert outdoes himself, demonstrating obnoxious, overbearing qualities. To avoid both extremes, and to contribute positively to the enjoyment of others, you must exercise self-control in social situations.

Concentration on others. That's really the key to social ease! Get your mind off yourself and onto those around you. (There again, you see the need for etiquette which is as much a part of you as your skin—so you can quit thinking about *your* situation at all.) The more time you spend thinking about yourself, the more miserable you're going to make yourself and everyone else. Concentration on nervousness just worsens the situation. So—forget yourself. Look around the room for someone who obviously is not a part of any conversational group; go to that person, introduce yourself, and initiate a conversation; concentrate on making your new acquaintance happy that he came to the party. Then move on to another "loner." Spend the entire evening in others-centered activities, and you will take home not only the enjoyment, but also the enrichment from the evening's experiences.

Social occasions and the clock. Sometimes when we're engaged in social activities we forget the passage of time. But forgetfulness makes things hard on others—namely, the host and hostess for the occasion. You know (or you will know someday) the inner weight of those stacks of unwashed dishes waiting for you after a meal or party. People who overextend their stay may have the best of intentions (demonstrating friendship); but the result is a hardship for the hostess. Etiquette prescribes that your staying time for a meal should be no longer than two hours and for a drop-in should not extend past one hour. It's *much* better to leave at a prescribed time, bidding farewell to hosts who wish you could stay, than to stay and have them wish you'd leave! And once you start to go, *do so*! Don't stand lingering over good-byes.

It is proper to offer clean-up help to your hostess. If she declines, do NOT insist.

Introductions. Introductions can present discomfort, because most of us have been taught the round-about formula of introducing someone *to* someone. It's much simpler to adopt a "name first" technique. Its principles are few and simple and are easily mastered:

In introducing a man and a woman, say the *woman's* name first. ("Mrs. Brown, may I introduce Mr. Smith?")

If two people of the same sex are to be introduced, mention the *older person's* name first. ("Mr. Seventy-five, may I introduce Mr. Fifty?")

If introducing two women of about the same age, mention the *married woman's* name first. ("Mrs. Green, I'd like you to meet Miss White.")

The *more prominent person's* name should be spoken first. ("Senator Smith, I'd like you to meet my mother, Mrs. Jones.")

When someone joins a group which is already conversing, mention the *newcomer's* name first; then proceed around the room or group in an orderly fashion, indicating each person as named (by a gesture, nod of the head, etc.) in order to help the newly arrived person put names with faces.

If you introduce people and then move on, leaving them to carry on a conversation with each other, give them a conversational aid. Such aids include the mention of a mutual interest, biographical item, occupational note, or *something* to serve as a springboard for their further talk, lest they be left standing there staring blankly at each other with the "Eeeek—what can I say to this stranger?" feeling.

Develop the habit of *introducing yourself* to those with whom you're not in frequent contact. *Never* be guilty of saying something "cute" like "I'll bet you don't remember me, do you?" That question rightly deserves a resounding "No!"; instead, you'll cause discomfort and embarrassment as your victim tries not to embarrass *you* in spite of your thoughtless approach. You will endear yourself to all if you form the habit of *never assuming you have been remembered*—give your name and, if necessary, the details which would help the person recall who you are and where he met you. When you encounter someone whose name you've forgotten, just politely ask it.

Meeting, speaking, and shaking hands. When a man and woman meet, it is the *woman's* place to speak first: that's one instance when a lady's initiative is not considered brazen. Likewise, the woman should initiate a handshake when being introduced to a gentleman. Men almost always shake hands in meeting; women seldom do. It is, however, definitely a sign of good manners to offer your hand when introduced: train yourself to do so. And by all means, learn to give a *good* handshake! Don't use a bone-crushing "I lift weights, too!" grip, but don't try for ultra-femininity with a limp, slithery, "dead fish" technique. A good handshake has four qualities: it is firm, elbow level, brief, and sincere.

Don't be an "instant buddy." That is, do *not* crash through the barriers of respectful formality upon meeting a person. Have the consideration and deference to *refrain from calling a person by her first name until asked to do so*. The exception, of course, is when dealing with those considerably younger than yourself.

Restaurants. It's always a special treat to get dressed up and go out for dinner in a restaurant. But there are some reminders about conduct for such occasions that can enhance your testimony as a polished Christian lady.

Upon entering the restaurant, the man checks his coat. The woman may either have him check hers also, or she may take it to the table.

The gentleman tells the hostess or *maitre d'* how many are in your party—so don't speak up when asked, "How many in your party, please?"

If the *maitre d'*, waiter, or waitress leads the way to your table, the woman goes directly behind him/her. However, if there is no one to show you to the table, the gentleman leads the way. The principle is that he is acting protectively toward the lady, "breaking the way" through the room's traffic.

The waiter seats the woman, or her escort does so. I've seen men plop happily into a chair held out by a waiter, not realizing he's proffering a courtesy to the lady.

If you are carrying a purse and/or gloves, they should be put on the floor, an empty chair, or on your lap—never on the table.

Suppose you and your escort have been seated at a table, served your water, and now sit with menus in hand; all at once you realize that the prices are much higher than you anticipated. Do you make a fuss, exclaiming loudly over "sky-high prices," etc.? Do you bounce out in an obvious huff? Either of those reactions will cast you in starring roles as Ungracious Associates,

Ltd. Instead, choose one of two actions: (1) search the menu until you can find an entry within your financial range, or (2) let your escort summon the waiter or waitress and explain in a quiet, mannerly way that you will not be having dinner there after all. You had looked forward to his/her service, etc., but . . . Then quietly make your exit.

Many really nice restaurants have their menus printed in a foreign language—notably French. *Don't* pretend you know what the dishes are and choose one via the eenie-meenie-minie-mo method. The proper thing to do is for your escort to ask the waiter to describe the various dishes. You will not only be doing the correct thing; you will also bring delight to the person serving you. Waiters in European restaurants take immense pleasure in describing the establishment's culinary delights.

The gentleman suggests two or three possible selections which lie within his price range—and the lady *never* orders beyond the price he has indicated.

The lady tells her escort what she wishes to order, and he delivers the message to the waiter/waitress. You need never speak to the person waiting table unless directly addressed. Of course, to respond to a "Do you want butter or sour cream on your potato, Ma'am?" by whispering, "Tell her I want butter, Herkimer," would be ridiculous!

If you are in a fine European establishment, be aware that the waiter will approach from your left and serve your plate item by item. He will expect you to indicate when you have received a large enough serving of each food. When eating in an informal restaurant, the basic rules of etiquette apply, but common sense will dictate necessary adjustments.

If a woman stops by your table to talk, your escort must rise and *remain standing until she moves away*. You do not have to do so unless she is a much older woman. It is never proper, however, for you to continue eating while someone stands at your table talking. Realizing that a meal must thus halt for politeness' sake, don't *you* be a tablehopping conversationalist!

On occasions when you are eating in a restaurant without benefit of an escort, leave the expected tip for the one who serves you: 15% of the bill. Women are notorious for not tipping or for under-tipping. If you are just too stingy to tip for the service you have received, *don't* leave a tract! (Christians are supposed to be charitable, remember?)

Church behavior. How are your manners in church? Do you leave them home? It's very easy to fall into too-casual conduct which is not only inconsiderate toward others but also irreverent toward God. First of all, you need to remind yourself that you go to church primarily as an act of *worship*. We modern-day Christians need to be impressed anew with the holiness of the God we love and serve! We have picked up a great deal of the world's cheapening, silly attitude that God is "the man upstairs." A new sense of God's holiness will shake us into realizing the beauty and privilege we have of worshipping Him as an act of love. That word, "worship," should set your attitude and actions for church conduct: quiet, respectful, and reverent at all times. Avoid gabbing, gawking, and giggling. How shameful are the circus-like actions seen all too often in the house of the Lord! Learn also to sit *still* in church services. Changing positions, crossing and uncrossing your legs, straightening your hair or hat, leafing through your Bible, drumming your fingers on the bench or chair arm—all of those can be maddeningly distracting to those around you: so much so, in fact, that they don't remember a thing said from the pulpit. Surely the Lord will not hold us faultless for such conduct.

Of course, as Christians, the friends who mean the most to us are those in our church family. That is as it should be, and the warmth of friendship and fellowship should be evident when we get together. But the visiting should be conducted *before* and *after* the church services.

General deportment. "Decorum" is a word seldom heard (much less *exhibited!*) in our day. Ideally, however, it should characterize every Christian woman. Decorum is simply propriety and good taste in behavior. Propriety demonstrates the principle that a lady *never* draws attention to herself by loudness of dress, voice, or action. Good taste will avoid such actions as scratching your head, touching your teeth, and cleaning or biting your fingernails in public.

How do you behave when you think you're anonymous? For instance, when you're in a city some distance from your own, and you're *sure* no one knows you. Do you drop your restrained behavior like a hot potato? Actually, the way you conduct yourself when you can claim anonymity is a sure mark of what you really *are*. And, after all, the One you are seeking to represent and to please above all others is always with you, always seeing, always listening. *That* is the reason our mannerly behavior must be constant in our conduct.

A lady always demonstrates respect for age. Whether the older person is a man or woman, you should rise, hold doors, carry packages, etc., as occasions present themselves.

What about gentlemanly assistance? It's great! Accept it—*graciously*. There are specific situations in which you can expect a man to assist you. On curbs and/or stairs he will offer his arm. (Take it *lightly*—don't throw him off-balance!) Getting on public conveyances he will let you mount the steps first and will offer his hand to give you balance; getting off, he will lead, then reach up to offer his hand as you descend. Crossing streets he doesn't have to offer his arm except in adverse weather conditions or especially heavy traffic, though he may do so. He will, of course, open doors for you. A revolving door offers him special challenge. He will lean past you, get the door started, then let you enter the first compartment, while he enters the next. He will also assist you getting into and out of cars by opening and closing the door for you. And, finally, he will help you get into and out of coats, jackets, etc. *Whenever* a man assists you, *thank him*! A woman who doesn't appreciate gentlemanly conduct doesn't deserve gentlemanly conduct. And that doesn't mean only your favorite tall, dark, handsome escort; it also means the nondescript little stranger who opens the door at the drugstore!

Finally, more unmannerly actions arise from thoughtlessness than from malice. Such is the case in blocking a doorway or aisle. Whether conversation or action stalls you in such places, think of those whose progress you're impeding, and *get out of the way of traffic* before continuing your business of the moment. Another type of thoughtless behavior is whispering penetratingly or talking during a church service, concert, etc. Save your comments until after the occasion. Other people are more interested in seeing and hearing what they came to see and hear than in your bobbing head and running commentary.

How do you behave when standing in lines? Do you exercise patience and good manners, or do you let your impatience make you grumble and shove? Remember that *no one* considers line-standing an interesting sport; and most are in as much of a hurry as you are. Don't add to their misery by your comments, and don't break in line.

Finally, avoid staring and glaring. For instance, if someone inadvertently bumps you in a crowded store aisle, do you dart withering glances toward the offender? Do you stare at conspicuously unfortunate people such as those who are crippled, crying, or very shabbily dressed? Realize, instead, that you can offer them a kindness—by allowing them the dignity of privacy!

The word which carries the loveliest accolade for a Christian woman's attitude, actions, and appearance is "charm." Yet the meaning of that word is much be-fogged and distorted. In all my reading, I found the most apt definition to be the following:

PRESCRIPTION FOR CHARM
—Author Unknown

For LIPS—truth, kind words, and a smile.

For EYES—friendliness and sympathetic understanding.

For EARS—courteous attention and wholesale listening.

For HANDS—honest work and truthful deeds.

For FIGURE—helpful and right living.

For VOICE—prayer, praise, and the lilt of joy.

For HEART—love for God, for life, and for others.

I hope that as you finish reading this chapter you have had two things distinctly planted in your mind: a determination to polish your social conduct and thereby enhance your testimony, and a realization that etiquette really boils down to *kindness—with style*.

Personal Pinpointing

1. At this point in my life, an unbiased observer would say that my manners count _____
_____the Lord Jesus Christ.
(for/against)

2. The most difficult thing for me to remember about having a gentleman seat me is _____
_____ .

3. I (do/do not) presently hold my knife and fork correctly when eating and cutting.

4. My most obvious way of telling the world I'm nervous is by _____ .

6. The statement, "A lady is a woman who lets a man enjoy being a gentleman" _____ ranks me as a lady in my present social conduct.
(does/does not)

Spiritual Balance

You can work from now till Granny's cow comes home and your sparkly "manners" will count for nothing if you don't let them spring from and continually be oiled by the grace of God in your heart. That grace will give you eyes that see others' sensibilities and needs, a heart that reacts in compassion and concern, and a spirit that moves you to be a *servant* of others.

9

To Close and Clinch

Perhaps you rationalize away any necessity for expending time and effort for self-improvement. There are several excuses commonly used to do so. But let's look at them and find out why they're not valid for a Christian woman.

Excuse #1: "I live in a one-store town in the sand flats of Outer Podunk. There's no use in polishing myself!"

As a first point of refutation, who says that small-town people don't deserve your pleasing appearance and mannerly conduct? What an insult to their importance as human beings! Second, who says you will *stay* in Outer Podunk? Many of us started in small towns, never dreaming that we would ever live anywhere else. But only God knows where He will lead any of us. It is important that we prepare ourselves so that our appearance, speech, and conduct will be acceptable and exemplary as positive testimonies for the Lord in any place, within any stratum of society.

Excuse #2: "Oh, I *know* how to look and what to do in special situations, if I have to. But why bother on a day-to-day basis?"

That attitude actually means that you only know *about* propriety—as a passing acquaintance, so to speak. But putting on a proper image like a coat is basically dishonest—for thereby you assume a role and act a part in order to make a favorable impression at certain chosen times. That certainly calls motives into question. And does Scripture ever condone dishonesty?

Excuse #3: "I'm going to be a missionary— why attend to good looks and manners when I'll be living among heathen?" Because, there ought to be some distinction between you and the savages!

Excuse #4: "It's unspiritual to want to look good and to put polish on my actions!" Only if you're a cave-dwelling hermit, Ma'am. Genuine spirituality translates into practical, balanced, consistent, compassionate *living*.

God *does care* about the appearance of that which represents Him here on earth. Have you never been struck by the marvelous detail to which God gave attention when He told Moses how to build the Tabernacle (Exodus 25-27)? The structure where He was to dwell that side of Calvary utilized materials and design notable for practicality, value, and beauty. Moreover, in giving instructions for the priest's clothing, He noted that it would be "for glory and for beauty" (Exodus 28:2). On this side of Calvary it is we individual believers who are at once tabernacles and priests. Has God changed? Is He grateful now for shoddy workmanship and cheap materials?

No, there really is no valid excuse against self-improvement. It is simply a matter of "whom do you love more—yourself and your ease, or the Lord and others?" Believers should exhibit the *best* appearance and speech, the *most courteous* conduct of anyone on this planet—for our Christ-centered hearts prompt us to it!

But refuting arguments is negative; let's move on to the positive aspect of the matter and consider the principles and practicalities discussed in this book as they apply to your effectiveness as a testimony for the Saviour.

It is of paramount importance to keep in mind, first of all, that *the scope of your social range marks the bounds of your witnessing's effectiveness.* Proper grooming, carriage, speech, and manners are acceptable on *all* social levels; impropriety severely limits your acceptability; and any level at which you are unacceptable means your witness is unacceptable. (There are, of course, exceptions when the Lord has bypassed His normal method.) Why, as ambassadors for Christ, should we hinder our ministry through selfishness, laziness, or inverted piety? Who *is* going to win the "up-and-outers" with whom the Lord may bring you into contact? A standard excuse often advanced by the upper classes for rejecting "religion" is the boorishness of religion's adherents. Sadly, that objection has been given too much validity by those who nonsensically claim that "hick-like is holy."

Second, *comfort contributes to communication*. Suppose you are a guest at a dinner sponsored and attended by the social leaders of your community. If you are jittery over your dress, grammar, or table manners, your nervousness will bind your brain and tongue, making it very difficult to communicate with others at the table. If, on the other hand, your refined actions and appearance are so consistent that they are as natural as your own skin, your freedom from tension will also be your freedom to communicate—and hence to witness for your Lord.

A third encouragement toward refining efforts is that *deference makes a difference*. The louder the world proclaims its philosophy "Do your own thing," the greater the Christian's opportunity to bear testimony through the difference evident in her deferential consideration for others. Self-discipline and kindness are so rare in our society that their consistent presence in a person's life draws attention and interest. That makes an effective springboard for Christian testimony.

Should you need further persuasion, go back to the epistles of Paul and note the emphasis he places upon his exemplary conduct under all circumstances. He was ever bold, but never boorish. He was able to say truthfully, "I was blameless in my conduct in all things." Why did he so emphasize this aspect of his ministry? *Because his conduct gave credence to everything he wrote and spoke.* So does yours—or else it belies all you claim to believe.

Although regrettable, it is a fact that the unsaved have higher standards for Christian conduct and appearance than do many Christians themselves. Believers spend a great deal of time and energy in mental gymnastics making excuses for a life-level as low as the world's. But an unregenerate person expects a "religious" individual to exhibit superior standards in every area of life. He *wants* and *needs* to see that there is a level of living which is clearly above his own. If the Christian flounders in the same crassness as the sinner, what inspiration, challenge, or hope can he offer? The superior life of a believer touches a responsive chord of yearning in the sinner's heart; the life of a mediocre Christian only causes disillusionment and contempt.

Terms and titles are cheaply purchased, or even stolen. "Christian" is indiscriminately appropriated for many individuals, institutions, and movements which are in opposition to scriptural principles. The only reliable way to identify that which is genuinely of Christ, therefore, is by a careful examination of motives, methods, and message in the pure light of Scripture. And, as you apply this scale of measurement to others, be aware that it is simultaneously identifying *you*. No one can be expected to be perfect in this world—but the born-from-above believer should certainly be scripturally selfless in his motivations, scripturally separated in his methods, and scripturally sound in his message. For a Christian woman, those things will be most effectively demonstrated *in her conduct and appearance*. God does not call us women to be the theologians or preachers in His scheme of things: He *does* call us to be a *living demonstration* of His Truth. That immediately cuts out the following:

Cheapness. I Corinthians 6:20: "For ye are bought with a price: therefore glorify God in your body, and in your spirit, which are God's."

Sexiness. I Corinthians 3:16, 17: "Know ye not that ye are the temple of God, and that the Spirit of God dwelleth in you? If any man defile the temple of God, him shall God destroy; for the temple of God is holy, which temple ye are."

Dirtiness or sloppiness. I Corinthians 6:11: "And such were some of you: but ye are washed, but ye are sanctified, but ye are justified in the name of the Lord Jesus, and by the Spirit of our God." How can such marvelous spiritual cleanliness be demonstrated by physical grubbiness?

Coarseness or inconsiderateness. Titus 3:2: "To speak evil of no man, to be no brawlers, but gentle, showing all meekness unto all men." Ecclesiastes 10:12: "The words of a wise man's mouth are gracious."

Efforts at self-improvement must be motivated by a desire to excel *for the Lord* and must be undergirded by His own power. As in every other phase of life, you as a Christian woman have as your supplier of strength and instruction the omnipotent, omniscient, all-loving God of the universe! And within you dwells the blessed Holy Spirit, Whose work (and delight) is to *refine* us by His pure fire.

When you lay aside this book, I pray that you will pick up a burden to let God's Word be used of the Holy Spirit to refine your heart and mind and to extend that refinement more clearly into every aspect of your appearance, speech, and conduct.

It is for the sake of your testimony as a thoroughly lovely Christian lady that this book has been written. May you lift your eyes from these pages to the blessed face of your Saviour, Whose matchless beauty we are to reflect. In, through, and for Him each one of us can and should have

Beauty and the Best